THE METAPHYSICAL CAT

Books by Gerald and Loretta Hausman

Dogs of Myth
Cats of Myth
The Mythology of Dogs
The Mythology of Cats

THE METAPHYSICAL CAT

tales of cats and their humans

GERALD & LORETTA HAUSMAN

for the evolving human spirit

HAMPTON ROADS
PUBLISHING COMPANY, INC.

Copyright © 2001
by Gerald and Loretta Hausman

Cover design by Grace Pedalino
Cover photo of Samir, the cat by Grace Pedalino
Cover photo of moon and snow leopard by PhotoDisc
Illustrations by Mariah Fox

For information write:

Hampton Roads Publishing Company, Inc.
1125 Stoney Ridge Road
Charlottesville, VA 22902

434-296-2772
fax: 434-296-5096
e-mail: hrpc@hrpub.com
www.hrpub.com

If you are unable to order this book from your local
bookseller, you may order directly from the publisher.
Call 1-800-766-8009, toll-free.

Library of Congress Catalog Card Number: 2001091196

ISBN 1-57174-256-5

10 9 8 7 6 5 4 3 2 1

Printed on acid-free paper in Canada

Table of Contents

In the Beginning, There Was Cat . . . Or Was There?

Cats are optical animals—always looking and learning and presumably thinking about what they're seeing. The question is, do cats *really* ruminate on things?

How presumptuous to ask.

Of course they do.

So do salamanders and skinks and worms and even microbes—and why shouldn't they? They possess life. To live is to think of that which is dear to living—life. Scientifically, this urgency may merely be called instinct. Yet call it what you will, the real question lies in the *quality* of the thinking being done.

What then is the nature of feline meditation?

The masters of the arcane, the mystics of old who gave the paradoxical cat a good philosophical going-over, so to say, generally agreed that she was thinking moment by moment, step by step—a spontaneous Zen puss always in the act of a new invention by way of movement, her body as much a part of her thought process as her mind. She thinks, therefore, in paws, eyes, ears, nose, whiskers, belly, and tail.

But who really knows if this is true?

We don't doubt that cats possess collective or unconscious memory, thoughts going back to the beginning of their—and our—time on Earth, but how well, we wonder, do they recall their lives as caretakers, guardians, healers, messengers, gods, goddesses, scapegoats, and devils? The following newspaper article from the Fort Myers, Florida, *News-Press*, raises more ticklish questions than answers about cat consciousness, especially in the area of collective memory.

Cats Attack Officers Trying to Remove Owner's Corpse

CAIRO, Egypt—Eighteen cats stood vigil for a week over the body of their master and attacked policemen who came to remove his corpse, police said Saturday.

Bahgat Mostafa Said, 63, a retired Egyptian civil servant, loved cats. He had eighteen of them, police said.

When Said died August 19th in his apartment in the

Cairo suburb of Heliopolis his cats rallied round meow-
ing and watching over him. A week later police came
to investigate a smell coming from the apartment.
They found Said surrounded by his feline family.

When police officers approached the body, the cats
set upon them, scratching ferociously, a police
spokesman said. It took the officers two hours to
remove the cats before they could retrieve Said's body.

In this book we've sought answers—mythological, historical, philosophical, behavioral—to all kinds
of speculations about the metaphysical cat. This is
the cat that lives next door, but also the one that lives
next door to the fifth dimension. We've reached out
to cat people all over the globe, pet lovers who
believe, as we do, that cats are intensely spiritual
beings. And feeling so inclined, these people have
shared their fantastic stories with us.

However, these are not tales from the crypt,
though some sound that way, but rather tales from
many dimensions, those close at hand and those far
away. This is the cat, cat of signs and psalms and
secret codes. Welcome then, the metaphysical cat.
The mysterious one who came late aboard the Ark
and left early on the Titanic.

Gerald and Loretta Hausman

The Cat Who Published Poetry

The other day at a talk we were giving, a student asked, "What was your first published work and who accepted it for publication?" Gerald answered, "The first work that appeared in print was a poem about a cat, that came out in *Cat Fancy* magazine. And the odd thing about how this poem came to be was that I was living at my parents' home and had made a promise with myself to give up writing. I was tired of getting rejection notices or not getting any notices at all, just silence and indifference from a bewildering host of editors across the country . . . so I'd decided to quit trying.

"However, that same night I was sitting at my desk and into my bedroom walked our family cat, a coon cat that weighed about twenty-nine pounds. She walked blithely into the stillness of the room and gathering her great fluffy tail around her, sat down and looked up into my eyes; and I swear that we had a conversation, and one that put me at a loss, for what she said made sense."

"Are you a quitter?" she asked.

"No, but I'm sick and tired of hearing the word 'no.'"

"If you were a cat you would hear it all the time."

"I am not a cat."

"We live in the same world, and it is a world of negatives. We cats really like to hear the word 'yes.'"

"We humans must enjoy saying the word 'no' because that is what seems to make us tick—telling others they can't do the things we ourselves would like to do."

"Most unfortunate . . . most human."

"So people who would like to write tell me that I cannot write."

"Do they write?"

"Yes, they write to me and tell me not to bother."

"Most unfortunate. But I wonder why humans can't be satisfied with being, rather than doing things all the time. It's a great advantage not to be possessed of hands . . . hands can do all manner of terrible damage. But our greatest advantage, as cats, is that people imagine that because we do not talk, we do not think."

"That doesn't solve my problem—wanting to write."

"Well, I am going to tell you, right now, to get busy and write something. I am going to ask you to write something about me, a portrait perhaps. How about 'The Portrait of a Cat Who Cannot Speak'? Yes, that's an appropriate message to get out and about. I will pay you handsomely for your work, don't worry."

"How are you, a cat, going to cough up cold hard cash?"

"I cannot do that."

"I didn't think so."

"But you will be paid well, nonetheless."

"In what kind of currency?"

"You will be notified and paid by check in no less than three months, human time."

"And I am to write a work subject to your approval?"

"That is correct."

"And it will be about you and the fact that you can't talk?"

"Or don't want to—it comes to the same thing."

"And for this, I will be compensated by check after three months have elapsed, correct?"

"That is right."

"How much will I be paid?"

"For a poem—you can write poetry, can't you?"

"Of course."

"Well, for a poem of ten to fifteen lines I will pay you seventy-five dollars."

"That seems like a lot of money for a cat to be throwing around."

"We don't throw money, we throw weight, if you get my meaning."

"You have connections, I suppose."

"We have ways and means."

"Very well, I'll do it. I'll write you a poem about your inability to speak, although you've just spoken surpassingly well, and I'll—"

"You won't do anything after that. Just write it and leave the rest to me."

"Fine."

So Gerald wrote a fifteen-line poem about the coon cat. I remember that the poem was a bit funny, but not really frivolous—it did no injury to his cat's dignity, nor to the tribe of tigers, in general—and he left it on his desk, neatly typed. Three months later, that poem was accepted by *Cat Fancy* and Gerald was paid seventy-five dollars.

The first thing he did was call home. He asked his mom if there was a poem on his desk and she said, no, why? He said that *Cat Fancy* was publishing one of his poems, a poem about a cat, but that he had never sent it to them.

She replied that Tatty, the coon cat, had brought the poem to her attention.

"In so many words?" he asked.

"Not in so many words," she answered.

"And so you sent my poem to that magazine and they accepted it."

"I suppose so. But you must give the credit to Tatty. It was her idea."

Some people might think that Gerald came from a very exceptional and eccentric family. And if you're one of them, you are absolutely right. However, I can

attest, as his wife, that this story is true as written. God bless Tatty, for she started us off. The only sad thing is that now we've let the cat out of the bag.

The Serpent and the Cat

Since the beginning, cats and serpents have been burdened under the same human concept of original sin. We've even heard people say that herpetophobia is genetically encoded in the human brain. If so, perhaps cats have something of this fear, too, because what cat doesn't recoil in arched horror at the sight of a snake or even something that vaguely looks like one?

Marjorie Kinnan Rawlings, author of *The Yearling*, writes,

> I believe that, contrary to Biblical implications, fear of snakes is not inherent in human beings, but is planted at an age so early that memory draws no

line for its beginnings. Fear is the most easily taught of all lessons, and the fight against terror, real or imagined, is perhaps the history of man's mind. The average man or woman says, and believes it, "I have an instinctive horror of snakes." Yet babies and small children, who might be instinctively terrified at the sight of a large animal such as a cow or dog, show no fear of snakes, but reach out their hands to them, and have even been known to handle venomous snakes without harm.

Our earliest mythology of serpents and felines comes from ancient Egypt. There, according to legend, the serpent of darkness was overcome by the male cat of the sun. Their daily battle accounted for day winning over night. This myth must be a part of the collective unconscious because Native Americans have similar stories, particularly the one about Bobcat and Old Woman Moon. She grows slender each time he playfully unravels her head strap. Thus explaining why the moon is reduced to a silver thread. The Egyptian version states that, when the sun god Ra lost his eye (the sun), it was found wandering on Earth in the form of a lynx or a desert wildcat.

Our Siamese cat gives wide berth to the serpents of our Florida pine flats. There are many poisonous species here, and she knows it. Also, some nonpoisonous snakes imitate the behavior of the deadly ones, so it's sometimes hard to tell—even for a cat—which is which.

We heard a weird tale the other day that illustrates the way many people feel about snakes. The story concerns a two-year-old girl who was admiring a bird of paradise tree in front of her house. She stepped so close to the palm that she was almost within the fold of its fronds. At the same time, her mother went inside the house to answer the phone. When she came back out, a frightening sight awaited her.

Her child was wrapped in the coils of a huge, glistening, black indigo snake.

The frightened mother screamed for help, and some neighbors came running, one of them carrying a machete. After it was killed, the indigo snake (which, by the way, is on Florida's Species of Concern list) was stretched out and measured. Head to tail, the unfortunate snake was eight feet long. It was also four inches thick.

The family was so unnerved by this experience that they dug the bird of paradise tree out by the roots and burned it. Underneath the roots, they said there were one hundred or more baby indigo snakes.

Is the story true?

Whatever parts of it are accurate, much of it also comes from the ancient logbook of biblical mythology.

Fittingly, the mother who witnessed the event swears "upon the Bible that every word is gospel."

Speaking of the Bible, cats are not mentioned but once in the Good Book, and even there, the reference is so vague that it might be bats or birds, and not cats at all. Serpents, as we all know, make a number of notable biblical appearances, often as a dragon.

The bird of paradise tree, the innocent child, the serpent—what a modern medieval allegory. But we make little of it, in terms of herpetology. There aren't any cases we know of where an indigo snake ever twined about a child or watched over a nest like a domestic fowl. Like most cold-blooded reptiles, indigo snakes have a lay-and-leave policy. Moreover, they do not victimize any prey that they can't swallow. Finally, their meal is mostly rats, which explains what the snake was doing there in the first place— looking for something small and furry to eat.

Our elder Siamese cat, Moonie, usually left snakes well enough alone, but one night when a Florida king snake, as pretty as a necklace, slithered into our living room, he turned into the avenging Sun Cat and slew the evil Serpent of Darkness before our very eyes. Interestingly, the markings of this nonpoisonous serpent, the Florida king, are nearly identical to the deadly, banded coral snake. It's just a matter of red and yellow, and red and black. As the old saw goes, "Red and yellow kill a fellow, red and black okay for Jack."

Could Moonie discern the glittery bands and know them for what they were? Why, when he'd never done so before, did he attack this particular snake? Other snakes have mistakenly slid into the house, which is open to the yard and the woods beyond, and he did not harm them. Well, not all humans have done the same and we have seen the remains of chopped up Florida king snakes lying out on the roadbed where someone—after flaying them—flung them. Of course, they were imagined to be coral snakes.

Cats, so inclined, can overcome snakes with stunning speed and we've rarely seen a snake get the better of a cat; though in places like India, Africa, and Asia, it happens regularly.

A *National Geographic* film we recently saw showed two black leopards attacking a water python. The snake had one of the cats in its coils and would've succeeded in killing it, but the mate was always there to break its hold. The great snake had no choice except to flee. However, even in the water the two sleek cats were at home. They caught the huge snake by the tail, and dragged it back to dry land.

This reeling-in of the reptile was a considerable feat because the snake was thirty feet in length and probably weighed hundreds of pounds.

The ancient enmity.

Day triumphing over night.

Some of us get the shivers just thinking about a serpent gliding through the grass. Our young Siamese warlord, Kit Kat, beds down in the palmettos so that only the burnt chocolate tips of her ears are showing. Every day she watches the pygmy rattlers come out of their holes and sun themselves on the pine needles. She chooses wisely not to fight them, or even accost them, and so the two live in a state of mutual respect, or perhaps, comfortable mistrust.

But if you don't think the ancient enmity is there, just dangle a ribbon in front of your housecat. Even a very old timer, a retired tom, will take the bait and attack the escaping tail of an imaginary snake.

The whole paradigm was once part of the original contract. Cats were given, by right, all vermin as their natural prey. This included snakes, rats, mice, rabbits, rodents, and all the random varieties of seed-stealing birds. Basically, all creatures that might harass the agrarian interests of farmers. Sadly, snakes kill the same vermin. They get no credit for this, however, and they are still hated and feared and killed with no remorse.

Have you ever seen a snake that tolerated, or perhaps trusted, a cat? We saw a four-foot anaconda face a scrawny little tabby. They stared at each other through eyes the color of gold. Unmoving, they lay at rest.

An entire day passed with neither serpent nor feline changing position.

They stayed that way until dusk, their eyes locked.

Grappling with the mind?

You could feel the tension between them. They lay inactive, yet ever alert.

Who won?

After eight hours, the snake lifted its oblong head, twittered its red tongue, and slowly—and as we imagined, humbly, or at least respectfully—withdrew.

The skinny tabby had bested an animal four times her size. But now she tiptoed, tail erect, into the kitchen and mewed for some food.

No wonder the old white-witch potions called for eye of cat and skin of snake. The two have such potency, such immediacy as imagery, such ancient standing as symbols of the Earth and sky.

The hot-blooded cat is day's golden warrior.

The cold-blooded snake is night's silent custodian.

And we humans still remember this four thousand-year-old battle, and we still shudder to think that day could fall victim to night. Or that the serpent might rise from his God-ordered, lowly dominion:

> And the Lord God said unto the serpent
> "Because thou hast done this,
> Thou art cursed above all cattle,
> And above every beast of the field;
> Upon thy belly thou shalt go,
> And dust thou shalt eat
> All the days of thy life.
>
> "And I will put enmity between thee
> And the woman,
> And between thy seed and her seed;
> It shall bruise thy head,
> And thou shalt bruise his heel."

Genesis 3:14-15

One thing we know—from personal experience—indigo snakes are friendly. One of them circled our house yesterday, as if to dissuade us from the tale we are writing. We went outside, and as the five-foot snake glided under a croton bush, we picked it up making certain to support its long tail end. Calmly, the deep blue-black serpent rested on us, its face upturned into the light, regarding us with such equanimity and beauty. The dark eye was fine and round, the tongue flicking, sensing our vibration.

After enjoying our sojourn with this huge, sculptural creature, and imagining him to be the very staff of Moses, we let him slide freely away. For the rest of the day, he turned up in various parts of our yard. And at dusk, Loretta found him in our laundry room—our doors being open to catch the sea breeze. He was hunting, and he paid us no mind but went from place to place in his easy, concentrated way, checking for a rat that had taken up lodging behind the dryer in our open garage.

Today, Kit Kat won't go out the back door without jumping two feet in the air to overleap the garden hose that is coiled there. The indigo snake that she wanted no part of—too big and too arrogant—lives on in the shape of that silly hose. There she sits, staring at that hose, glaring at it . . . menacingly . . . thoughtfully . . . wisely.

The poor serpent's ultimate indiscretion was offering Eve the apple. Yet, according to Dominican scholar Matthew Fox, this paradigm is not original sin but original blessing.

Animals, in our experience, are seldom good or bad, but a mixture of all things great and small, good and evil. In the Everglades once, we knelt by a flowing stream and counted water moccasins. We stopped after we got to thirty. These supposedly territorial snakes made no movement toward us—and we made no untoward gesture at them. Yet we were only inches apart.

Another territorial and supposedly ferocious animal is the fisher. This is the small cousin of the wolverine. Fishers of New England despise cats, and kill them on sight, or so we've heard. However, like the wolverine itself, the animal is much maligned. The fact is, creatures act in accordance with their own laws, as well as the natural laws of the species. The other day, we heard about a deer in upstate New York that attacked and killed a pack of dogs. We wonder why humans can't accept that animals are exactly like us—given to individuation. The sweet-tempered dolphin is not always so. Neither is the serpent so suspicious and dangerous as our own ignorance of its ways.

The heavy-hided alligator takes blows from the press on a daily basis in Florida, and—well, try to envision this true-life picture. An old, white-bearded man was fishing in a remote Everglades canal alongside a twelve-foot alligator. The man was sitting with a bamboo fishing pole, and the alligator was right there with him, watching and waiting for his common share. They'd been fishing that way, the old timer said, for many years.

Maybe the ancient enmity ought to be seen as the old harmony. Let the snake discard its worn skin and let the cat drop off its extra fur. Let us all walk anew as if the day and night were one and the tree of paradise were watched over by an indigo god.

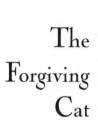

The Forgiving Cat

Every so often, a child in our household asks where cats come from, and why some have tails and others don't, and why cats do the amazing things they do—such surprising things as, after being lost, walking thousands of miles to hone in on their home. "How do they do that?" our granddaughter asked us.

We tell her the question is probably unanswerable. No one really knows how lost cats get home. But there are some stories that tell of the cat's beginnings, stories which explain, to some extent, why cats make their home with us in the first place.

Off we go into the world of mythology and some of the most beautiful whoppers ever told—Aesop,

Ovid, Kipling, Van Vechten, and Twain. But are these stories so far-fetched, or are they far-flung from another time? Actually, myths are the sacred oral history of humankind. The collective memory of man, woman, and animal. They are true and accurate, in the religious and the sacred sense, and sometimes quite true from the scientific perspective as well.

Take, for instance, the myth of the cat's coming to life.

"A lion sneezed," says the old storyteller, "and out of his generous nose came a cat—not such a big one either, but a tiny one." So, that's how the first cat came into being, and it all happened on, or in, the Ark. Who was the old storyteller?

Noah? All of us? None of us? The lion? The cat?

Mythology doesn't say who said it first, it only says that it was said.

Some myths have a real, arguable, historical background. This one, for example, about the Manx cat: In 1588, a ship from the Spanish Armada was sunk off the coast of the Isle of Man (between Scotland and Ireland), and two *rumpy* (as in tailless) cats swam for shore. There were, it seems, some witnesses to the event.

Other, later, reports say the ship was wrecked on a reef off the Calf of Man, and on board were two full tailed cats who made it to shore, but couldn't climb up the slick rocks to higher ground. Legend has it the twosome wore off their tails while going up and down the slippery rocks.

Then there is the more ancient myth of King Arthur. Supposedly, he banished from Great Britain a famous female pig named Henwin. On the way out, Henwin did a most amazing thing. She gave birth to bees, barley, and—you guessed it—a cat. This feline swam to the Isle of Man and took up residence there, and no one questioned its quirky, quarky tail because the people of Man were so used to looking at rabbits, with which their little island was so well stocked. (If, by chance, you ever called your bob-tailed Manx cat a pig, you were not wrong—mythologically speaking, that is.)

And what, if anything, do the old myths say about cats *with* tails?

Mainly, that tailed cats are crafty in the ways of the world.

Such myths say that the long-tailed cat's facility for catching mice is as great as her vanity. The tail, as it were, increaseth Her Royal Image.

All in all, the tales of the furred and tailed point out that, though cats may teach us their craft—how to be crafty, they also show us how to be better people.

They instruct us in being smart, rather than just clever. Yet no matter how great the mythical cat teacher, we humans have failed miserably at being feline.

Alas, though they may have taught us something about vanity, they have never taught us how to be beautiful—not since Egyptian times, anyway. And so, the mystery of feline grace remains a secret that mascara and eyeliner cannot hope to imitate. This singular beauty—whether tailed or tailless—transcends breed, blood and bone. It matters not what kind of cat you have—alley cat, farm cat, city cat, suburban cat. Any kitty is an unearthly entity of perfection. Born beauty, marvel to behold, regardless of type. Perhaps that is the ultimate myth to explore . . . that of the space cat. (Many Egyptian tales tell us that cats are ethereal and dwell in the heavens.)

So, the cat without pedigree and minus any authenticated bloodline, despite purges and persecutions through the ages, has, by beauty alone, managed to keep her dignity intact. Whatever she was, whatever we might want her to become—she'll only consent to be what she is. And that is a sublime creature of *purrful,* powerful, perfection.

Where, the poets ask (Christopher Smart and William Blake among them), does this excellence come from? Some of our myths say that the cat's love-liness is born of *forgiveness*. We do not get such a Christ-centered image of the cat unless we harken back into the Essenes, the esoteric teachings of Jesus. What these particular myths say is that the cat, as kit-ten, is kind and comforting. Baby Jesus, they say, was amused by one and he adored the mother that bore such beauty.

How, we might ask, can the proverbial cat forgive humanity for the purges of the Middle Ages when the so-called Christ-centered cat was cast into oblivion?

Has Bast, Pasch, Puss, the Goddess Cat, forgiven but not *forgotten?* Has she forgiven us for murdering her by the millions? For burning, baking, and putting her in the ash barrel? For feeding her to dogs, hogs, and birds? For kicking her over the centuries? Has she turned the other cheek after we, literally, once used her for a live football? Has she gotten over our hanging her by the tail, setting her afire, and putting explosives inside her?

For heaven's sake, how could she? How *could* she trust us at all? The charitable miracle is that she has done this very thing.

So, the next time your cat flashes a "vengeful eye" or looks cattily at you, remember this—she never plotted to kill you for the color of your hair.

Remember, she never burned you up during the Inquisition!

Instead, remember well her pact, for it has lasted all these countless centuries. Cat's well-kept promise was to catch mice, or any other vermin, so that we should be able to make our daily bread. As the official guardian of the grain and queen of the corn, she ensured our livelihood, and she does so to this day. Yes, she is still humbly at work, mousing and musing, never moping, always working in our behalf.

Do not think it is genetics, training, or instinct—though it may be all of these and more. Once again, our myths point out that cats favor human companionship; they love us for being what we are and what they are when they are with us. It is a divine alliance, a partnership—a mystic, talismanic association that, so our graveyard poets say, goes beyond the grave into the other world, a world in which the cat is more than just conversant.

Well, with or without tail, headless, tailless—as in the Cheshire—but never mythless, Puss is with us to the end. And she will purr forgiveness into ten thousand wrongs. So said Jesus when he walked catlike upon the Earth.

The most forgiving cat we ever knew was a Maltese who had been terribly abused as a kitten. By the time we got him he had been given a succession of drugs including LSD. Brain damaged, dropped out of two-story windows, left to die in lonely forests, beaten and abandoned, Greyman, as he was called, finally found his way to our doorstep. He liked nothing better than climbing up on us and sleeping on our chests and purring the night away. The only problem was this: When a synapse short-circuited in his misfiring brain, he would jump straight into the air, land on all fours, and run for cover. Once, he rocketed up towards the roof and scrambled out of an open window and ran straight down the outside stone wall of the house.

We went after him, of course, running half-naked through the pine forest of the old estate where we were staying. We found Greyman at dawn, curled up in the arms of a marble Nereid, a sort of Earth angel who once was part of a lovely turn-of-the-century fountain, now long dry and draped with velvet moss. What a picture Greyman composed, lying so soft and enchanted, and in such repose in the cool, dead marble arms of a blank-eyed Romanesque angel. We took him back to bed as the sun rose, and he fairly roared a purr of thankfulness at being found.

One amazing thing about Greyman was that he learned to open doors. He walked in beauty like the night, mantled in moonsoft, fragrant, silver-gray fur. We never knew how he did it—how he opened doors—but we always heard the click, and then he entered the room so pleased with himself. This was a far cry from his vaulting and running down walls.

We loved Greyman, but one day he opened a dozen doors and, in a perfectly calm frame of mind, walked away into the forest never to return.

Although it has been thirty years since we saw Greyman in the flesh or fur, he comes back from time to time. There is always that door-click, and then the throaty purr, and we know Greyman's returned to say thanks. Oh, what frightful colors and jagged chasms he must have seen in the nightmare alleys of his mind when he lived with us. There was no holding him then; he would tear you to ribbons. But afterwards, when the lightning in his head stopped sputtering, he always made his peace and said, the only way he knew how, "Thank you for caring for me . . . I know that I am not what I ought to be."

The other night when he came home for a brief visit, we saw that he had lost his cat shape and was human again. "More time," he said, "more time," as he pressed our skin with his healing hands. His face, when we could see it in the bluish translucence that was his shadow form, was like that statue buried in the hidden woods of the old estate. Yes, he was a stone angel, softened by thirty years or, perhaps, thirty seconds.

Noah's Cat

In the beginning, Noah bid all the animals come aboard the Ark. And they came, the winged, hoofed, pawed, and clawed. Those that slithered and those that slunk. And all were welcomed by the man, Noah.

However, just as he was about to button things down for forty days and forty nights . . . just as the great rain was about to come down upon the land, Noah paused and scratched his chin.

He wondered, "I saw them come two by two, all the animals of the Earth. I saw the lions and the lizards, the owls and the shrews . . . but did I see them *all*? Did I see each and every animal that lives and breathes? Did I, by chance, leave anyone out?"

Now the rain was raining down and the rivers of water were filling up every crevice on Earth. The Ark was starting to rise, its prow pointing upwards towards the sky.

"I had better check," Noah said, "check one more time, and make sure I've included every animal that has hooves, claws, paws, and scales—but not fins—on the Ark."

So he opened the hatch to see if anybody was left in the rain. There was nothing there but darkness and wetness. And there was no end to it. So he closed the hatch.

"Well, I suppose I didn't leave anybody out," Noah said.

Then he heard a little squeak.

"What's that?" he asked, opening the hatch again.

In the pelting rain he saw a cat.

Not a panther, not a lion. Just a little wet cat.

"Come here, Puss," Noah coaxed.

The cat, staring disconsolately at the open hatch, backed up.

"Come inside," Noah said.

The cat crouched down in the rain.

Noah got an idea. "I beg you," he said. "Come within and see what I have built just for you—for you alone."

The cat's ears perked up, and she came a little closer and peeked inside the Ark.

Satisfied that the smell was dry straw, but puzzled by all the other animals reclining on it, the cat held back. Then with a flick of the tail, she said to Noah, "You did say this was just for me?"

"Come in," Noah begged. "We're getting damp."

But the wet cat caught the eye of a winking camel.

"Are you okay in there?" the cat questioned with uncertainty.

"To be sure," the camel said.

"Very well," said the cat, and she went in . . . well, almost all the way in. Noah, thinking she *was* all the way in, dropped down the hatch.

At the same time, the undecided cat changed her mind again. She whirled about to hop back through the hatch—but not before the wooden lid slammed shut and cut off her tail.

And that is why some cats, to this day, haven't got a tail.

It's also the reason why all cats mistrust doors, gates, hinges, and hatches.

And that isn't all, there's more to it . . . yet another story with a slightly different twist of the tail.

You see, Noah was counting heads. He was going along, counting and saying, "Two elephants, two doves, two snakes, two mice,"—and so on and so forth until he noticed that there weren't *two* mice, there were *ten*. "Pardon me for saying so," he said, "but that's too many mice."

Now the ten mice didn't like hearing this. Away they scampered into the straw and disappeared. "That won't do," Noah groaned. "We can't have you mice overrunning the Ark." Then, to all assembled— the great and the small—Noah asked, "Who will help me diminish the mice?"

No one said anything. So he said, in much plainer terms, "Who will cut them down to two just like the rest of you?"

He glanced at Bear, who looked away.

He stared at Seal, who merely smiled.

Then he laid eyes on Lion, who said, "If you wish to lessen the mice, you must have a cat."

Noah asked, "Are you *not* a cat?"

Lion said, "I . . . a *cat*?"

"Well, aren't you?"

"Certainly *not*," Lion said. "I am a Lion."

"Then what am I to do?" Noah asked.

Whereupon Lion took pity on the poor man. He put his thumb over his left nostril, and he . . . *sneezed*.

And out of his nose came a puff of smoke that turned into a cat.

"Meeow," cried the cat, a welcome sound if ever there was one.

And even before Noah breathed a loud sigh of relief, the smoke-colored cat ran to the straw and pounced on a mouse.

"Ah, this is good," Noah granted. "But there's only one cat—and all the rest are in twos." He looked pleadingly at Lion, who drummed his claws and arched his neck and . . . sneezed once more.

And then there were two smoky cats aboard the Ark.

There was a he to go with the she, and in no time at all they brought the mice people down to two, a male and a female. But, then the mice people made more mice, which is why cats, today, are always on the prowl and must be on their toes and engaged in their own special business, which—as we all know, is the catching and dispatching of mice.

And that is where the story ends . . . but not quite.

Sometimes, you see, we get the feeling that our own home is an overloaded Ark. And maybe that is why we like Noah tales so much; they seem pretty down-home to us and to a lot of other people we know, who also have houses like ours—filled to the rafters with creatures of all kinds.

The other day our daughter, Hannah, who works for Big Brothers, Big Sisters in Miami, was at a workshop in which the group leader asked each person to tell "two truths and one lie." The idea was to guess the untruth and thus to learn more about the person. Well, Hannah chose her family's overloaded Ark for her "truth," but everyone took this for a lie. They said afterwards they just couldn't believe she'd grown up with so many animals. What she said was, "I lived with four dogs, five cats, six birds, two hamsters, two rats, and lots of lizards and snakes."

To us, however, this seems like a moderate number of animals for a home. We are always opening the hatch for another newcomer. As a boy, Gerald had possums, raccoons, flying squirrels, gray squirrels, snakes of all sorts, ducks, rabbits, dogs, cats, fence lizards, alligator lizards, alligators, iguanas, and skinks galore—and always room for two more, as his mother liked to say.

Once, a friend brought six rattlesnakes and stored them in a burlap sack in Gerald's father's home office. In the morning when his secretary started typing on her electric typewriter, the wastebasket replied with a righteous buzzing of its own.

She typed, stopped, listened. Then she crept over to the wastebasket and peered inside. She saw a crocus bag bulging with something sinuous—where-upon she backed off in trepidation, and hollered at the top of her lungs.

Presently, our house is peopled with two Great Danes, a dachshund, two cats, a blue-fronted Amazon, lots of Cuban anoles (chameleons), a black racer, an indigo snake, and three long-necked turtles. There is a tree rat living up in the attic and just recently a possum vacated the apartment in back of the dryer. . . .

Those of us who live aboard overloaded Arks seem to have our own unorthodox mythologies. They come with the territory. Stories grow like fox grape vines all along the fence. Here's another: Gerald's mother once put out her hand on a clear blue summer day and a mockingbird landed on her index finger. She kept the bird on her patio for a week. Then she let it go, and it flew away and made a nest nearby. We once knew a boy who had a pet fly that took up residence on his right arm for one whole week. It would fly away for spells, but it always returned. He fed it sugar water. At the end of that week, the fly left and didn't return.

Kindness to creatures seems to grow exponentially in certain families, and it is passed along the gene pool of time and place and, certainly, of tale. After years of telling, adding, and subtracting, it's hard to know what really happened the first time around; a family mythology is like that, full of rough-edged truths, bountiful, natural, wayward rambles in the world of nature. The pith of these stories is usually quite accurate, but like Hannah's seminar, the truth is hard to hear sometimes, especially if it contradicts the rules of our own personal suspension of disbelief.

We love animals, no doubt, and they love us in return; and it's always been that way. The other night, we had a family of screech owls that whinnied us to sleep (yes, that is the noise they make). Anyway, one evening, we went out and they regarded us with their studious, brown, round, owly faces, cocking their heads the better to see us close up—and we and the owl family were almost touching noses.

What a wonderful exchange of views it was—the owl children looking studiously into our eyes and us gazing into theirs. Each of us looking, and not moving. If only more of our tribe, the fractious humans of this over-peopled planet, would stop, look, and listen—as they used to tell us in school—and do no more than that.

For, in looking, and not judging, there is so much to learn. Last spring, one of our long-necked turtles, who lives in the freshwater pond which is only a couple yards from the house, kept coming round by our studio where we were working on a new book. The door was open, and this large mocha-colored turtle with a six-inch stretch-neck appeared at the screen and seemed to be asking us for something.

After a while, Gerald and I—fearing she might be hurt by one of the Great Danes gamboling about the yard—returned her to the pond. However, she scrambled out, and was back at the screen staring at us a moment later. At that point, we relinquished our work and went outside to find out what was going on. This time, seeing how earnest we were, she took us to the rear of the house. There, under a big Washingtonia palm, while we were watching, she deposited a clutch of eggs. No question, that was her urgency—she wanted us to know precisely where she was burying those eggs, so that we, as landfolk, could watch over them. We think we did our best—there are more baby turtles in the pond this year.

The strangest night visitor that ever came to our house was a creature the size of your thumb. This happened twenty-five years ago and we remember it as if it were yesterday. We were living then in the Berkshires of Massachusetts. We had a farmhouse on a hill, and it was winter—a snowbound night of thirty-some degrees below zero. The famous night not fit for man nor beast.

Gerald and I were sitting in front of the warm woodstove when there came a high twittery squeaking at the front door. When we opened it, a blast of frozen air cuffed us in the face. But there at our feet was a little shrew with a long, pointed nose and extraordinary whiskers; he was sounding off in tweets and whistles of rage, and fairly hopping up and down.

Well, he came dancing into the kitchen, and we closed the door behind him. He never stopped squeaking until—after some trials and errors—we fed him some raw hamburger meat. This he devoured at an appalling rate, and he ate a frightful amount, and yet it was probably equal to his body weight—and that's exactly what a ground shrew needs to stay alive, its weight in meat every three hours. Eat-and-Run, I called him (Gerald called him Hopping Mad) because directly after he ate, he demanded to be let out. Our striped Persian cat watched the shrew eat and depart with supreme feline disdain. However, she didn't lift a paw against him.

Cats and shrews are mortal enemies. Still, cats generally won't eat them—they're bitter fare for the feline, not to mention how hard shrews are to catch, and what a fight-to-the-death they put up when caught.

 That night, there must have been one of those Ark-like spells about the house. The snow was a white ocean that hemmed us in and held us aloft. A cold, yellow moon bore down, gilding the frozen landscape to a white-gold froth. We imagined we were afloat, drifting across the white night on a winter sea. The warm wooden hull of our ship was a creaking host that night to one crazy, piping shrew, and the cat, Krebs, was mannerly and kind, knowing that it is not *always* necessary to be quickest to the mark.

The whole time the little animal gorged, Krebs lay with her hind feet tucked under her belly and with her front paws lined up for a chin rest. Her green eyes looked strangely sympathetic. She knew her job was mice, but this puffed-up little poof of person was not one of those. He was a trembly furor of energy come in from the cold. Yes, surely *he* was something else. Some other order of creature.

And so are we all, each and every one of us. If only for a winter's, or a summer's, mystic moment of suspended judgment.

The Goblin Cat

Herodotus stated that the law of ancient Egypt required a man to shave his eyebrows as a sign of mourning when the cat of his household died. Yet this was only one of the customs at the time of Bubastis's glory, the time when cats were not only praised but worshipped. There were even a few wars presided over by cat generals.

The feline lived high on the pyramid of life during the days of the Pharaohs, and she ruled all realms, physical and spiritual. As for the noble Greeks, they were so busy copying Egyptian arts and sciences—geometry, astronomy, and philosophy—that they didn't have any time for cats. A pity, too, because they tried to solve their mouse problem by having weasels for pets.

Weasels are fond of killing, and that's putting it lightly. Actually, they delight in killing well, and just about all Greek domestic animals were fair game—and game fare—for them. Moreover, as we know from Aesop, the Greek weasel was a particularly sly and creepy individual.

So, what did the Greeks do?

They did what they'd *always* done . . . dispatched spies to Egypt. And these spies came back with—you guessed it—cats! These, in time, solved the problem of the weasels, but by then the Egyptians were on to the Greek theft, and they sent spies to steal back their cats. Moreover, there was a law in Egypt that made the taking of a cat a capital offense.

How devoted were the Egyptians to their felines?

Very, very.

In fact, the Persians once *borrowed* a bunch of cats from them and, led by Cambyses I, won a war by holding these felines in front of the Egyptian army which outnumbered them ten to one. The mere sight of their cats in the hands of their enemies caused the Egyptian forces to surrender.

So, to keep this from happening again, the Egyptian spies rounded up as many stolen cats as they could, and the Greeks were forced to honor the owls of Athena, in the hope of reducing their outrageous mouse population. When Alexander conquered Egypt, he tried to eliminate all the cats that were underfoot, but the populace wouldn't have it, and the Egyptian mau lives on to this day.

According to cat historian Margaret Cooper Gay, in her book *How to Live with a Cat*, "The war that ended Egypt's greatness was started by a cat. A Roman who lived in Egypt accidentally killed a cat. The enraged Egyptians killed the Roman. At the end of a long war Mark Antony killed himself, the asp bit Cleopatra, Egypt became a Roman province, and the cat ceased to be a god (goddess) in the valley of the Nile."

We don't really know where the line is drawn in the sand to separate misty fact from foggy fiction; but in Europe, anyway, it's clearer. There, the feline rose and fell with the times, but her true lineage descended directly from the ancient kings of Egypt. When Fergus, the first king of Scotland, was crowned one hundred years before the birth of Christ, he bore, believe it or not, Egyptian blood. His family had carried cats to the Highlands and so the Scottish cat (named for Scota, Fergus's ancestor) wasn't just a granary guard in Scotland, but a mascot, motto, crest, and the definitive aspect of the fighting warrior. County Caithness is still called "the County of Cats."

Angus Mackay (*The History of the Province of the Cat*) remarks that "The Duke of Sutherland is still the Diuc Cat, the Duke of Cats. And the bagpipes of the ladies from hell still caterwaul like wrathful toms."

In the Netherlands, cats appeared quite early, too. The Romans describe a tribe they met at the mouth of the Rhine. This tribe called themselves "the Cat People." Their place, not surprisingly, was Katwyk, otherwise known as Cat Town.

In old Ireland, the Celts originally banished snakes with rhymes. However, once they got a hold of cats, the snakes were chased off by paws and claws. Saint Patrick, the great owner of wolfhounds, got rid of both cats and the snakes—thinking them of a similar kind—with a magic spell of his own. Legend says, however, that the cats he banished went right back to Egypt where they believed they would be treated with respect.

O, what a tangled web we weave. Some of the earliest Irish churches feature not saints, but cats! Carved stone cats. Thus, we know that even Saint Pat couldn't evict a creature as cunning and as pervasive as the feline. Some historians agree that Celtic cat lore goes back to the first days of Ireland, and that the original cats of the Emerald Isle probably came from Africa.

Myth or fact?

We don't know.

We *do* know that the six or seven hundred-year eclipse of cats, which is conveniently but sometimes mistakenly called the Dark Ages, were anything but dark. They were fire-bright, actually. Would these times have been munificent, minus the witch-cat persecutions? In other words, if cats had killed the bubonic plague-ridden rats, would the Dark Ages have been called the Light Ages?

Before the Inquisition, the cat cults of Europe thrived and made magic. One thousand years after the death of Cleopatra, the women of the Rhineland met in the moon groves and prayed to their cats. They worshipped Freya (from whom we get the name Friday), goddess of the North. Freya's chariot was drawn by harnessed cats, and it arced through the heavens with a cold blaze of feline fury.

Fertility rites crept through Italy and France on quiet little cat's paws. The Cat of Valhalla was praised and honored; whiskers and claws were sacred talismans. The shadow of a cat cast upon a moonstone was considered very powerful magic, indeed.

But all this passed, as we know.

The feline fall from grace came in 1484. At that time, Pope Innocent VIII decreed the death of cat-worshippers and witches. The broom went up in the blaze, too, for this was the thing that women held over men. It was thought to be phallic, and when ridden, was thought to produce a singular ecstasy untaught and unenhanced by a man.

The rest is too banal to go through again—all the burnings, beheadings, flayings, and skinnings. Cats were dipped in oil and set afire. Such atrocities were popular as late as 1800 in Europe and America, and one could argue that they go on today.

There is more to say, however, on the demise of the cat as goddess. During medieval times, cat worshipers could escape the stake—and still worship cats. How did they do this? Cat lovers let go of their cats and created an all-new cat person, one whose identity wasn't so obvious. In the midst of the mindless persecutions, the cat's persona became a godling. And a cat, minus the fur and flesh, was born—a mythical cat. His name was *kabouterje*. Or *colfy*. Or, more commonly, *goblin*.

Here was a cat creature with more powers than before. A link between the old sacred ways of worship and the dark, denying days of the Inquisition. Here was a supercat—a changeling. A being catlike and human, who appeared in the form of an aggressive and clever little man.

Arguably, he wasn't a cat at all. Certainly not in flesh. And perhaps not entirely in spirit either. Yet the cat *was* in the colfy and the kabouterje, and the lovely, ugly goblin. And in them, he would live forever. He would moan in the eaves of houses and he would hiss before the fire. Sometimes, up the chimney he'd go, bursting into a fireball when the occasion arose. He would also tie himself into knots of yarn just for the fun of it. And he'd feed on his favorite food—mice! He would live in vacant barns and play impish tricks on all who thought they could see him in the straw. Hah! He knew he couldn't be seen.

Oh, but the cat-goblin was playful, and wonderful.

Best of all, as he was made of pure fancy, he was immortal. He couldn't be burned, flayed, or drowned. The goblin was untouchable by mortal hand. However, he lived as surely as any creature that the mind has fashioned out of the fertile ore of the imagination.

Today, he—not she—still lives in storybooks, myths, and legends. His only enemy? A real, flesh-and-fur cat. Anyway, that is what the old tales say.

Our great aunt Gladys used to cringe whenever she heard Gerald recite Carl Sandburg's cat poem, "Fog," the one that starts off, "The fog comes on little cat feet . . ." She shuddered when she heard it, then shivering, she would say, in a high-pitched reedy voice, "Oh, you can have 'em, those nasty little cat's feet!" Whether she was a true ailurophobe, a cat hater, we don't know; but we suppose not, for she dearly loved all animals.

Perhaps the goblins had got Gladys. Or maybe she didn't like Sandburg's metaphor (in fact, we've never seen a cat fog), but in any case, she was the first person in our family to seriously object to cats in this way . . . in an almost goblinesque way.

Our cousin Kyle was just the opposite—a cat lover from the word go. Kyle's household is always crawling with cats, the overflow pouring into the New Hampshire woods where she lives with her husband, Don, who is also a cat person.

It was Kyle who first introduced us to *catspeak*, the language some humans find advisable to use with those certain cats which are partial to it. Catspeak is feline patois. Part English, part whisper, titter, and tatter. It can't be described adequately, but Kyle can speak it; and her cats—certain members of her tribe anyway—listen attentively to it and they reply in a similar style, with little cooey throat noises.

Kyle and catspeak remind us of the fact that she thinks cats are capable of almost anything. One of her cats, a pariah of sorts, lived high above her kitchen cabinets—an aerial beast who answered to no one but

Kyle and Don, having turned her back on the rest of her furred family. The most peculiar cat of Kyle's had a strange habit of walking into fire and was nearly burned to death on several occasions. Kyle used to say that this feline had survived many witch burnings and was still proving her immortality, her 9,999 lives in Heaven and on Earth.

Well, even Kyle, with all of her mystic feline leanings, has a limit. It's the one that most of us—if really put to the test—also have. We are speaking now of the unease we feel, even as cat adorers, when Kitty brings home Mousie and crunches her up and down. Not long ago, while visiting Kyle in the Berkshires, one of her leading cat heroines went out and got a bunny, then two, then three. These were newborn rabbits still suckling the blue milk of their mommy, and the sight of them wounded, dismembered, and dying was more than any of us could take.

Goblin time had come upon the twilit haven of the lake cottage where we had all grown up, and we shivered like Aunt Glad and remembered the shuddery saying, "A rabbit just jumped over my grave." And we wondered, then, in the failing spring light with baby bunnies dying all around us, why it had to be so.

Uncharacteristically, Kyle upbraided her cat, Mo. In fact, she did not stop. She chased Mo under her car and threatened him with murder and mayhem. Nor did it end there: Mo got fussed at and even spanked hours later when he came in empty-pocketed and rabbit-weary that night. Next day, more of same. Well, we were burying dead bunnies and it was awful, but Mo was only genetically to blame . . . right?

Again, this is where the goblins come in. They appear unobtrusively, we believe, sort of egging on the helpless feline who is at their bidding. Isn't that so? The paradigm, in real life—rather than literature and mythology—is that the cat hunts for us and tries hard to please us, and when that fails, she, he, or it goes goblin. We've seen it time and time again.

Our own beloved Kit Kat, unable to gain our full attention, waits for us to fall asleep and then attacks our Great Danes, who lie at the foot of our bed. She enlists them in a subversive kind of nocturnal war-fare, which is solely and selectively designed to make us mad. If, however, it doesn't work and we do not rise to the occasion, she then goblins-off into high gear by jumping up to the windowsill and pur-posely entangling herself in the vertical blinds. These contraptions come down with a terrible tum-bling—cat ensnared within—and before we can free her on the floor, she explodes to safety, to an under-

couch enclave where she is
utterly beyond retribution.
More gobliny maneuvers ensue
until we oust her into the night,
but it still isn't over. After devil-
ing the animals outside, she

lights on the window ledge by our bedroom and
sharpens her claws on the delicate and expensive
screen. That always gets her in. (No, we don't have
a cat door . . . yes, we are planning to get one, though
it may end up being a mosquito door in these sub-
tropical climes.)

Goblins do exist, don't they? If not historically,
histrionically. If not materially, immaterially. So that
the expression ought to be—"What's the matter, goblin got your tongue?"

The Cat
as . . . Cat

We are not done with the goblin yet; almost, but not quite. The crazy little cat gnome had so many names in Europe, and we've only identified a few of them. The Dutch called him *kabouterje*; the French, *gobelin*. The Germans, *kobold*; the Russians, *colfy*. The Welsh, *coblyn*; the English, goblin.

The Scandinavian people, being farther away from the Inquisition, had no great need to abandon their beloved puss, and as a result, their goblin was less disguised than some of the others. Known as *smierragatto*, buttercat, he was the spirit of bounty, the guardian of bread, butter, milk, and the thing behind all of these, money. In Finland, the buttercat was known as *haltia*.

He lived in the rafters and brought good luck, and did household chores. When a Finn built a new house, he always took along the rooftree and a shovelful of ashes to please the buttercat, who drank milk and, when visible, looked exactly like a real cat. Perhaps this is why cats to this day still prefer ashes to cat sand. Those readers who have fireplaces and cats know what we're saying.

All in all, these Nordic cat goblins were viewed mostly as fantastical cats rather than altered humans. However, the goblins were also handy-dandy shapeshifters and could change forms at will. Their mythology reveals them to be house-guardians gone sour, good-natured goblins whose amusing games have suddenly turned sinister.

Once the Inquisition was over, human nature required a new creation—one both fanciful and fun loving, and also a little diabolical. The good goblin got to be an evil gnome. He still had catlike qualities—large eyes and an appetite for cream—but now he had an attitude, an agenda. He liked to inflict woe upon people and things, and his worst enemy became his old persona, the cat.

Feline mythology shows that cats have a dual nature. When the persecuted cat no longer needed to be a fictitious goblin, she had to have a greater role than that of plain old mouser. So she became a warden against evil, a huntress of the unseen. She was an insurance policy against goblins, which in time had gone from being half-cat, half-human imaginary creatures to seemingly real-life hominids. The role stuck and held fast over the centuries, and it still holds true today, for we still believe in things that go bump in the night—Bigfoots and Nessies and Goblins.

In Stephen King's *Cat's Eye,* the good cat conquers the bad goblin, though the cat is blamed for the evil the goblin does until he is cleared and proven to be trustworthy. For instance, in the film we see the goblin sucking the breath from a baby. This ancient superstition comes from many sources, but the old goblin was always capable of breath-sucking; and cats, who were common visitors to cribs (they were stationed there to look out for rats), got the blame for stealing baby's breath long after we'd forgotten why they were there in the first place.

In America, the cat fared ill with the Puritans. However, by the beginning of the eighteenth century, every Scottish peddler carried cats and kittens along with the tinker's tools he toted in his wagon. Cats, he knew, were benign, and because of this, they had quite a lot to do with colonizing the continent. It happened like this.

As woodlands fell to field, the cat found her place in and around the cabin, chasing rats, field mice, rabbits, chipmunks, and snakes. Her value as sentinel was no mere myth. Her use, as the peddlers knew so well, was as necessary as a Kentucky long rifle. Once again, in the years prior to and during the westward expansion of America, the cat was a cultural hero. The good Gaelic influence may have had something to with this, but there were other factors.

On this continent, there were forty groups of rodents with seven hundred and fifty subvarieties, all waiting for a farmer to come along and raise a crop. There were wood rats, pack rats, and a host of other natives. In addition, there were the critters that came over from Europe—black rats, brown rats, roof rats, and many kinds of mice. However, squirrels were the worst of all. In 1749, Pennsylvania Colony alone paid bounties on 640,000 gray squirrels. Need we ask why cats were valuable?

In more modern times, the cat is still not forgotten for what she once did so well—and can still do when necessary. According to Margaret Cooper Gay, at the turn of the century there was a plague of rats in Memphis, Tennessee. "Rats attacked people on the streets and bit babies in their cribs. The town had become almost uninhabitable when a man across the river in Arkansas advertised rat traps guaranteed to catch a rat a day, price one dollar. The frantic people of Memphis swamped him with orders—and got cats. They were furious and there was talk of jailing the rat-trap man for fraud. Before the talk developed into action the cats had cleaned up and Memphis was fit to live in once more. They still like cats in Memphis."

Today, the cat's mythic stock is as tall as her tail. Just look at the casts of cats on television, the theater, and in books and films. There's *Catdog*, *Animaniacs*, *Sylvester and Tweety*, and *Tom and Jerry*. Disney cats run the gamut from bristle-faced Black Pete in Donald Duck cartoons to Dinah in *Alice and Wonderland*. Also, let's not forget the *Aristocats* and *Oliver and Company*, to name a couple more, and the *Sailor Moon* felines, Luna and Artemis.

In the theater, one of the longest-running musicals of all time was *Cats*, which had a run of eighteen years. In the newspapers, Garfield has grown greater as an icon than Cat Woman, the catty antiheroine of *Batman*. No question, cats are in—they haven't really been out for a very long time—they outnumber dogs in the average American household, and their popularity is constantly growing.

The reason for this may be mythical—we seem to believe there are more goblins than there used to be.

The Cat from Heaven . . . and Hell

Our friend's Persian is all snowy, a subtle cat whose elongated tail is an animated ostrich plume, always whistling this way and that. She has a brother who is also Persian, a jet-black, wondrous cat, no less dramatic in gesture and appearance. Together these two make a prodigious pair. The black one's name is Lucifer—he's an aerial feline who takes flight after moths and other summer-winged things. If the mood suits him, Lucifer can jump as high as a ceiling fan. In fact, on more than one occasion, he's broken one of these by hanging onto the whirling paddle.

Lucifer's mephistophelean manner is accented by the way he greets you—tail up and high and curved into a question mark. Face looking right up at you, and playing the old tempter to a "T." It's not just his bounding at fans that makes him impish, or his leading looks of deviltry. His lamp eyes seem to tell a thousand tales of a thousand other lives, but it's something else about him that intrigues us.

Black cats do have some rather heavy mythology. Going way back, there's the Teutonic myth of the hell cat, or, correctly put in German, *helkat*. H. P. Spofford, whose work appears in *Cat's Company*, by Michael Joseph, once said she knew a helkat whose "nightly journeying among the stars got him a hurt foot slumping through the nebula of Andromeda, while getting his supper at a place in the Milky Way, hunting all night with Orion, and having awful fights with Sirius. He got his throat cut by alighting on the North Pole one night coming down from the stars."

The feline described here was also named Lucifer. One of his least endearing and most puzzling habits, Spofford wrote, was that he constantly sucked on his own tail. Pardon the pun, but she tried to curtail Lucifer's fixation by putting a little pepper sauce on the tail-tip, which of course didn't work because Lucifer developed a taste for the particular brand she used: Hell Fire.

Next she dipped his balding tail in bitter aloe, but that didn't work either. At the end, she gave up and just let Lucifer suck his tail to oblivion. Another thing about Lucifer—he had a very strange appetite. Normally he was a moderate eater, yet on occasion he'd snatch a huge T-bone off the table, and then he'd devour it on the floor like a starved panther. Nor was this all—he was an inveterate fisherman. Quite often he had a fish in his mouth that had just been plucked from Mrs. Spofford's private trout stream. One day she saw him with eyes all aglow, fish in mouth, growling. There was a look in his eyes that said, "If you try to take this fish away from me, I will kill you and eat you, too."

It occurred to Mrs. Spofford that her Lucifer was a beast of myth, an incarnate helkat—not a devil or a daemon—but a creature of a different order.

Right she was, too. Because the helkat predates our Christian cat myths. And as Mrs. Spofford says, "It began with the old fellow who put his hand under the cat to lift her up, and she arched her back higher and higher until he found it was the serpent . . . I always said they [cats] were possessed of spirits, and they use white magic to bring their friends together."

Notice that the cat she refers to is female, not male. Was the original concept of the devil, then, female?

The answer's yes.

In Teutonic mythology, the Middle Earth was wrapped 'round by the Midgard Serpent. Above this, the gods built their mansions in the sky. Yet in the lower world there lived all those people who had ceased to live. This lower residence was alive with the *undead*, but it was not viewed as a place of punishment, as was later assigned by our Christian conversion of Hell.

The Germanic word was, in fact, *Hel*. It was the name of a goddess, a sovereign of the underworld. Fittingly, her face was half white, half black (yin and yang). In Scandinavia, the goddess Hel was the daughter of Loki, the trickster. Later on, in Christian mythology, Loki turned into Satan, or Lucifer.

So Hel, the Teutonic goddess, was the blood relation of the Devil, who was male. Furthermore, the great serpent surrounding Midgard was one of Hel's friends, and as we know from reading earlier versions of the Christian Bible, there are serpent-dragons there, too.

Now we know why the black cat with an arched back adds mystery but not menace to the October pumpkin night called Halloween. The cat's arch aims at the stars, the realm of Asgard and the twilight gods. At the same time, rooted upon the Earth, her hiss is that of the Midgard Serpent, who binds the Earth— this is why we say *earthbound*.

The coils of the Midgard Serpent were believed to be just like the serpentine tail of the black cat. All in all, these myths are a potpourri of old belief systems which are greatly entangled. They represent the collective unconscious of the human race, and they stretch so far back in time that we have lost track of them.

Our daughter, Mariah, when she was five, explained to us that cat magic could be imbibed by human beings. All you had to do was "take a pip off a cat." What was a pip? Well, by this she meant that you touched the cat's cold nose with your index finger, and then you touched your finger to your own nose. The result was something of an electric impulse infusion . . . magic.

Mariah came by this arcane knowledge all by herself. Curiously, her daughter, Shai, who is now five years old, traipses about our house and takes pips from our cats. Like mother, like daughter. The belief in cat magic runs strong in this odd family of ours. However, this is a very ancient thing, as we've been saying. Cat's pads were once used to heal the eyes. Cat guts were once "read" to divine the future. Wet cat noses were thought to reveal ecstatic visions.

When Loretta's father, Roy, was suffering from Alzheimer's and we were caring for him in our home, he kept his distance from Kit Kat. He told us one day that, in his view, this was a dangerous beast. We asked him why he thought so. He explained that Kit Kat changed into a Florida panther. He said he'd seen her stalking the pine flatwoods at night. In the dark, he said, she grew large, surly, and wild.

One night while sitting on our porch, we heard a cat—or what sounded like one because of the claws—fall from a pine tree. The animal landed hard and loud—*whump*. We waited at least an hour for the creature to take its first step. We presumed it *was* a cat, and a large one at that, and it refrained from giving away its position for a long while. When it walked off into the dense palmetto thickets, we knew from the sound that it was a large animal. Palmettos, being dry and papery, caused the creature's departure to be as noticeable as if it had been a four-footed man.

The following day, a neighbor who owns a mango farm said that he had seen a Florida panther crossing Burnt Store Road, not far from where we live. But Loretta's father gave us the knowing nod when he said the old panther was afoot again—he'd heard it, too.

Out in the palmetto scrub, I sniffed the spears of bent-down plants, and rummaged in the woods trying to pick up the trail, but there was none.

Well, the cat is out of the bag, as they say, and the pips are passed around to one and all, and delivered

accordingly to old believers—those who stay up at night listening for padded feet on soft turf. The big cat is yet with us and she has furnished more American myths than almost any other animal in North America.

And that redolent magic illuminated the first scientific books of beasts, the bestiaries, wherein the panther was equated with Christ. Her breath was his wisdom . . . even her urine was thought to turn into precious gemstones.

Myth? Magic? Memory?

Freya, the Midgard Serpent, Apep.

Large or small, domestic or wild, the cat is a creature of the imagination whose real presence is all things at once—this is what turns the housecat into a tiger . . . and the tiger into a kitten.

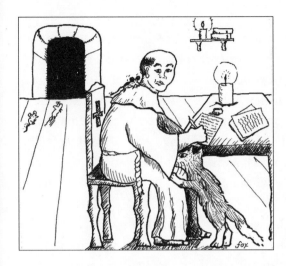

The
Monk's
Cat

"Pangur Ban," the first historical cat in Europe, was a feline of high sensibility, honor, and devotion; not at all selfish, as the earlier fables seem to insist.

Pangur Ban appears as an individual of a species, both like and unlike our cats of today. The illuminating verse is written by an anonymous ninth century Irish monk on a copy of St. Paul's Epistles at the monastery of Carinthia in Austria, and gives us a unique insight into the charming and uncalculating metaphysical cat.

Unlike cats in fables or bestiaries, Pangur Ban was a real animal whose telepathic thoughts were communicated to his late-night friend, the nameless monk and scribe, who left behind a small legacy of very wonderful words.

The poem that follows is translated from Gaelic into English, and it's more than a thousand years old. It is the survivor of many Viking raids, as well as foul weather, fire, flood, and forgetfulness; and, somehow, by some unknown miracle, it made it to our millennial doorstep.

One might wonder what an Irish monk whose writing was in Gaelic was doing in a mountainous monastery in Austria. Well, the Celts came to what is now Austria in 390 B.C., the year in which they also conquered Rome. Articles of their conquest are still being discovered today. They were lovers of cats, the Celts. They even went into battle with cat masks over their faces, thus to invoke the shamanic power of the cat, so that their fighting would be effective, elusive, and wreak havoc upon the enemy.

International storyteller Bert McCarry was greatly influenced by the legend of Pangur Ban, she says. Claiming she first heard it as a child, she actually met the fabulous cat one day in Dublin. "On a visit to the Irish Folklore Department at University College," she told us, "I came down a long staircase into the lobby and faced a larger-than-life statue of a monk and his cat. The monk sat on a high stool, and was writing upon a slant-top desk. I knew before I read the inscription under the statue that the cat at his feet was Pangur Ban."

What does this cat suggest that haunts our imagination after all this time? What is its meaning?

Is it just a cat imitating human behavior?

Hardly.

Pangur Ban, the poem, is proof that cats have something to say. Something that is almost, but not quite, within the scope of our understanding. If we meditate upon it, might we decipher the meaning of Pangur Ban? Might we decode the mystery of the talking cat who, so far, has not deigned to speak?

Let the poem speak for itself.

For Pangur Ban
(translated by Gerald Hausman)

I, and Pangur Ban, my cat
A common task we are at;
Hunting mice is her delight,
Hunting words I sit all night.

Often times some mouse will stray
Out my sleeve in Pangur's way;
Often times a thought is set,
Caught quick in my mind's net.

The two of us work as one,
Day moon, night sun.
I who study moral law,
She the keeper of the claw.

The Life and Times of Pangur Ban . . .

Being the Illustrious History of a Real Cat Who Was Much
Smarter Than the Monk Who Made Him Known to the World

The monastery lay deep in the mountains. There, late one spring as candles guttered on the night wind, Brother Patrick copied St. Paul's Epistles. Pangur Ban, his faithful cat, was tired of batting moths that fluttered around Brother Patrick's dancing taper. He, too, sat on a stool, bored.

"Have you not something else to do?" Pangur asked. He could, indeed, talk—not with his mouth, but with his mind.

Brother Patrick replied, "For the love of St. Paul, can't you see this is sacred work I'm doing?" These words also came across the silences of the night. They were unspoken, but perfectly received by Pangur, who was a large, bluish feline with a full face and whiskers. His fur was a good deal more plush, not to mention cleaner, than Brother Patrick's well-worn robe.

"All work is important to a cat," Pangur said philosophically. "For, of course, we cannot do work ourselves.

By the way, a little diversion might improve your penmanship."

Brother Patrick felt prickly under his woolen robe. Sometimes Pangur annoyed him with his sacrilegious suggestions. "And how," he asked, "might I divert myself?"

"You could try writing 'The History of the Cat,'" Pangur mused. "That, at least, would be more playful than this tiresome epistle."

"Cats haven't a history, as you claim."

"Oh, you're wrong there, my friend. We've saved the day many a time . . . not to mention the night."

"The night?"

"I told you not to mention the night," teased Pangur.

Brother Patrick sighed. "Name one little time when a cat saved anything of importance."

"The last time I saved you from losing your temper," reminded Pangur.

Brother Patrick shook the big sleeves of his robe. He wagged an accusatory finger at Pangur Ban.

"I have been patient since the day I was born, so don't tell me otherwise."

"I won't," said Pangur. Then, he added, "I watch you scratching impatiently—not always with your pen. One imagines the Devil's own mice are crawling up your sleeve. And do you call that patience?"

"I call it rubbish," said the irked monk.

"Quite so," said the cat.

"Why am I passing thoughts with a cat when I should be working?" Brother Patrick took a deep breath and exhaled noisily. The flame of the candle trembled. "It must be the lateness of the hour, or some crumb of cheese," Brother Patrick muttered.

"Or, perhaps, the mouse up your sleeve," put in Pangur.

"What mouse?"

"The one that is looking for that itchy little crumb that missed your mouth at supper."

Brother Patrick peered into one of his cavernous sleeves.

"I see nothing," he told Pangur.

"How could you? You're a man."

After saying this, Pangur sprang from his stool. He dived into the cave of Brother Patrick's right sleeve. Out of his left sleeve came a mouse, which jumped to the floor. Pangur exited the left sleeve in the same manner as the mouse. Presently there was a scuffle on the stone floor. Then, with the mouse in his mouth, Pangur hopped back up on his stool. "You see how it is?" he mumbled. "You monks have your heads in the clouds while your sleeves are full of mice."

Then Pangur raised his upper jaw and prepared to devour the mouse.

"Do not crunch those live little bones in my presence!" said Brother Patrick, agitated.

"All right, I won't," said Pangur. He let the mouse go and it scampered back up the sleeve of Brother Patrick.

"Oh, dear," moaned the monk. He started scratching himself all over. "How shall I ever get another word scribed?"

"Let me do my work," suggested Pangur Ban, "and you shall do yours the better."

Brother Patrick was now hopping about on one foot and the other, trying in vain to shake loose the mouse.

"All right," he said. "Go in and get rid this pesky mouse."

Pangur gave Brother Patrick an expressionless stare, but he didn't move a whisker.

"That's an order," said Brother Patrick.

Pangur shrugged. "As you wish, Master," he said sarcastically. Then he did as bidden. After the mouse was dispatched, Brother Patrick went back to his candlelit copying of St. Paul's Epistles, and all was well. However, Pangur had one more thing to say.

"Please, Brother Patrick," he said, "do not forget to write 'The History of the Cat,' even if it is so short a thing as a single verse, for it is I and my kind who have been faithful to you and your kind since we both plied our trades 'neath sun and moon."

"That has the ring of a poem," Brother Patrick smiled.

"Then write it so," advised Pangur, "and make me, and my kin, justly known for our service to humanity."

And now you know how we've come to have the wonderful poem, "For Pangur Ban," which you now realize is no simple twist of Irish whimsy, but lines to be plumbed by the best of minds; these are lines written by man, but *thought* by cat.

Dear Pangur, we know you well, though your sleep of twelve hundred years goes on and on. We humans are still stupefied by cats that speak, believing so adamantly in our singular vocal perfection. What animal dare lay claim to human speech? And if you should ask why cats are quiet, think of this—if they were to speak as freely as Pangur did, they'd get nine hundred years of bad luck, and they know it. It happened once, it could happen again.

The Cat and the Hereafter

One doesn't need a garden of catnip to attract a cat. The fact is, cats come into our lives when we *need* them the most, but also when we *want* them the least. Anyway, they're usually around, just out of sight. One of our favorite come-hither cats was a mysterious beast named Fang Clamp. He got that name because he liked to bite people. Moreover, when he bit into someone's flesh, he wouldn't let go until his jaws were pried apart.

Fang Clamp was a tomcat in the prime of life, who weighed about twenty pounds. A gray tabby with large, green, luminous eyes, he showed up on our friend's doorstep one morning. He was yowling. Or, to be exact, yodeling. For the length of his stay, he drove away every cat lover in the neighborhood.

No one liked Fang Clamp, and for obvious reasons. He did, however, draw forth a pack of malicious back-alley dogs, all of whom he summarily trounced. Fang Clamp was invincible.

His favorite food was lettuce. It was strange to see so great a cat dining pleasurably upon romaine, red leaf, Boston Bib. He enjoyed the best, crispest lettuces, and he never allowed a wilted green to enter his mouth.

In short, Fang Clamp was an awful cat, devoted to biting every gentle hand that touched him. He was a fussy eater and a earsplitting yodeler. In the end, he sank his teeth into the leg of a man wearing a leg brace. Outraged at the imperviousness of the brace, Fang Clamp yodeled violently, turned tail malevolently, then departed, never to return.

The Buddha once received a package from an enemy who desired to take his life; Shakyamuni returned it, unopened.

Fang Clamp was such a package. Whatever dark soul inhabited that great, gray-furred body was greatly agitated, and six months of gratis greens didn't, in the slightest, cure his menacing malaise.

After he'd bitten practically everybody, he went away—where, we don't know.

Some packages, fur included, need not be opened. This is not to say that all cats come with restless souls, but merely to suggest that cats are susceptible to spirit visitations of all sorts. Not to mention personality disorders.

But the magic of the cat remains. Fang Clamp, whatever he was or wasn't, brought with him a chain of bad events and miserable vibrations that lasted for months. Practically everyone who came in contact with him experienced some kind of "darkness."

In the British Isles, cats were once capable of darkening the sky and changing the weather. The phrase "raining cats and dogs" comes from this archaic, but at one time practical, idea. You can find plenty of references to it in Shakespeare's plays, particularly *The Tempest*.

The feline is as mutable as the moon. That fanciful tail and blazing eye, and that flowing, snake-like form have always aroused suspicion, superstition, envy, and disgust, as well as a heightened sense of magic.

Although we've grown to accept that the cat-witch is a false and foolish archetype, we're still entertained by the notion that cats are often visited by "traveling souls" looking for a final home, but not really finding it. As a culture we believe, as did our ancestors, that cats are capable of anything. Said another way, they are the vessels of the spirit world.

In ancient Egypt, the feline was known as Mau, which means seer. The feline symbol was the all-seeing eye of Horus, the hawk-headed god. We are still convinced that cats may be clairvoyant, clear-seeing Maus.

From the earliest of times, cats have always been designated psychic messengers, and they share this distinction with owls, with whom they have a strong facial affinity. The feline mythos—seeing that which we as humans are incapable of seeing—is more popular today than ever before.

Yet, as we honor and revere the cat's powers, we also shiver a little at their actual performance—as in the case of a cat like Fang Clamp. Is this just a carry-over of ancient superstition? Consider that the word superstition comes from the Latin. Its implied meaning is "survival," so, to be superstitious is to be survival-oriented, a skill that our techno-society still regards highly. To pass from one end of life to the other, and thus to survive death itself, might be the greatest of all possible virtues that a human could achieve. This is certainly the case in all of our most profound and deeply affecting myths—from comic strip characters like Superman and Mighty Mouse to Orpheus and Faustus.

The Egyptians believed that cats possessed the ability to aid humans in finding the next world, the world that comes after death. Partly, the myth of nine lives stems from this old belief of cat immortality.

But along with awe comes wariness, and although we pay homage to ancient mysteries, the cat being one of them, we are cautious and fearful of going too far with this.

Interestingly, when the Greek goddess Diana was banished, she selected a cat's body for her immortal vessel. Then, having assumed her feline form, she took refuge in the moon. The cult of Dianism was the worship of the All-Mother, Cat.

No wonder we associate cats with shapeshifting and the spirit world; our oldest and most revered traditions taught us well, and we haven't forgotten. Another interesting fact is that cat mothers are thought to be the most perfect of all—our modern myths, often true, show how mother cats rescue their children from burning buildings with no fear for their own lives.

These stories challenge us to rise to a higher plane of consciousness. We admire the cat mother, we emulate her. And we stop just short of worshipping her.

If you believe that spirits pass fluidly through the revolving doors of life, then it's not difficult to imagine that cats are a likely portal of entry. Mythology says that their door is always open to that lonesome traveler, that wayfarer from the hereafter. What of the other "designated" animals who share this mythology—those other enchanted ones? The owl, the crow, the raven, the wolf, the snake? These creatures have the same aloof intelligence as the cat—and they share the same mythological history of recrimination, persecution, and worship. All have languages too, vocalizations rich in meaning and intonation.

Here we are suggesting that cats and the beasts of superstition are ready subjects to be read into, to be molested in a way, by mythology. Woe unto those whose feather, fur, and fin are black. Or who move in silence during the night. Or who regard us with suspicion or possibly derision. The wolf and the cat are foremost in this—or shall we say, "foemost"? And all of the above-mentioned have been accorded the ability to shift their shape and turn into one or the other of their ilk—for instance, owl to cat, cat to snake. A shiver goes up the spine—is this true?

If you follow mythology, as well as natural science, you discover that the thing all of these animals have in common is that they like to be out of range of human perception. Yes, even the cuddly kitten likes the dark cave under the bed. But all cats enjoy  keeping us, their so-called keepers, at one remove. And this, more than any-thing, infuriates our sense of kindly humanity . . . we take the cat into our home, and look what she does: She treats us like help, she sleeps apart—but worst of all, she *thinks* apart!

Regard the cat who stands up for her rights. . . .

We remember the feisty Persian that warded off all warmth and affection. Her name was Nicodemus, and the thing Gerald liked to do was pick her up and kiss her on the head. Nicodemus tried to resist and could not, considering that Gerald was fifty times her size, until the day she became a clawed avenger, and with a single swipe of her paw, she sheered his cheek and lip, and the blood poured forth, and he never, ever picked up Nicodemus again . . . a lesson well-learned.

Nicky stood up for her rights.

Pity the poor cat that has to defend her dignity in such a way. Nicky was no vessel of vindictiveness; she was no Fang Clamp. A cat is, sometimes, ofttimes, just a cat. An offended cat is twice that, and more. And this has less to do with metaphysics than manners, but just the same—know your cat and whereof she cometh.

Cat's
Night
Out

The song says, "The cat came back the very next day; the cat came back because he wouldn't stay away." It didn't matter how many times the cat was lost or even killed, she always returned, good as new.

We have often wondered why.

Dogs come and go, but in the end when their lives are over, they accept their journey and don't return. But cats are another story.

What is it about the feline persona that binds it to our heart in such a way that this spirit—or energy, or whatever you'd like to call it—moves visibly through the veils of worlds unseen and unknown?

What is it about the cat that keeps her with us after her life on Earth is over? She is not coming back to retrieve us, nor is she possessed by another spirit.

We are talking of the cat ghost that stays around the house because it can't stay away.

Well, there are of course spirit dogs. European myths tell of them, and we too have mentioned dog ghosts in several books, most notably *Dogs of Myth*, which recounts the tale of the ghostly retriever. Hounds, in particular, are spirit beasts, and this myth goes back to the days of King Arthur and the quest for the Holy Grail.

However, there's no comparison with cats: cats come back to haunt. There is the tale, for instance, of the preacher and the cat, told here as it was once given to us in Natchez, Mississippi.

There was once a preacher who bought a house haunted by cats. He didn't believe in ghosts, but his first night on the premises, he sat on his newly painted verandah and, with Bible in hand, he leaned back in his rocker and exhaled contentedly. "If this place is haunted," he thought, "surely it's haunted only by beauty."

The night seemed to sigh. Then the preacher heard a prowl, a growl, and a most unseemly yowl. Glancing to his side, he saw a pretty little Persian kitty. When he scooped it up in his lap, the kitty changed into pale moonlight. The night stirred. The preacher heard a mewing and looked at his feet. This time he saw a full-grown Persian cat that resembled a white chrysanthemum. As he stroked its fur, the sultry cat vanished.

Next there came a lion-like snort. The preacher looked in astonishment. A lion was seated at his right, and on his left there was a wildcat with a bobbed tail. Then they too vaporized in the sultry, southern air. The humid night smelled of pecans and oaks and curtains of kudzu. The darkness breathed, exhaling a musky odor of cats.

Suddenly there was a loud growl in the camellias. Off in the twisted oaks under the phantom mosses, a leopard coughed. The preacher smelled the rusty stink of pelts, as slinky shadows appeared on the lawn. Red eyes embered and burned through the opaque moonlight. The cats stalked on, and the violent accent of the night was augmented. The preacher shut his eyes, and a series of searing, orange stares followed him into the private darkness of his head.

Out on the blue lawn, the foggy shapes of predatory cats converged. They were coming slowly to get him; he could feel them stalking him. Thrusting his Bible before him, he dashed down the cat-crazed stairs and walked out through the catty-cornered hallway. Across the growling yard he went, holding his

Bible out like a talisman. All around him, the indistinct shapes of lions materialized out of the night.

And so he left that place, never to return. Nor did he ever preach another sermon, for, as he put it, "the cat got my tongue that night, and never gave it back!"

We once had a Persian cat named Krebs who detested dogs from the moment she was born until the hour of her death— and thereafter, too. All of her life, she did battle with the *canidae* family, and had many scars to prove it. Krebs lived a long, long time. In the end, she resembled a shell of her former self, a husk of dry skin with the orientation of a cat. A simulacrum of cat.

We buried Krebs and put a stone mound over the grave.

That night we heard a cacophony of curs.

Somehow, every dog in the neighborhood assembled at midnight and unearthed Krebs' modest little gravesite. And they dragged her poor body all over the countryside. We searched the neighborhood up and down and discovered the meager portion that was once Krebs. We'd named her after a character in an Ernest Hemingway short story called "Soldier's Home," about a man who couldn't be killed and returned home desolated by war. That was Krebs the cat, all right. She fought with dogs all her days, and died with her legend intact. Yet now that she was deceased, the dogs sensed her spirit was on the prowl, and somehow sought further, and final, revenge.

We buried Krebs again.

And again.

We buried that poor cat so many times that, in the end, she was nothing but four hard paws connected by sinew to a skeleton and some fur. However, no matter what we did, or tried to do, to make the final rites stick, they came undone. The dogs found her and flung her to the winds. The next day, after the midnight orgy of cat flinging, we discovered what was left of Krebs—finally just shreds of cat's down—in a tree, on a bush, under a porch.

At last, we decided to put the scant remains six feet under the earth. After we did this burial, we rolled boulders on top of her grave for markers, and over these, because Krebs was such an indefatigable road warrior, we placed hubcaps. Twenty glistening hubcaps formed a crown of sun-glistened glory over the site.

And that stopped the canine marauders. The deed was done, let peace last, everlasting. Ah, Krebs, you can sup on peace without measure and without end, amen.

Some years went by, five to be exact. We returned to the old gravesite, and found: the hubcaps gone, the boulders rolled, the earth riven by pawmarks. Yes, they'd come again on the nightwinds. They clawed the poor place from top to bottom, and left no particle of sand untouched.

What happened? What was all this about?

Emily Brontë, speaking of Heathcliff, once said that the strong cannot be contained by life, or death, and so must live on in whatever world they choose. And, thus, the cat came back the very next day, the cat came back because he couldn't stay away.

We once asked—begged is a better word—our favorite Siamese, Moonie, to haunt us a little on moonlit nights. He blinked his promise, died, we buried him, and that very night—keeping his pact—his spirit returned and walked through our house. We heard him yowling and singing in the curious, calliope-sounding, Siamese way that goes through your whole body. He did this for about a week, then left and hasn't been back. We think he had better timing than Krebs. But both cats were a testament to life after life.

Holy Cats!

We heard about "leap of faith" felines at a monastery on the shores of Inlay Lake in Myanmar (Burma). It seems that the sacred Burmese temple cat, a monastic feline bred for centuries in isolation, was the subject of a legend. During the Burmese war of 1885, a British officer gave an account of the subterranean temple of Lao-Tsun. Within its labyrinthine chambers resided a master and his cat.

The sacred cat was said to be possessed of such magic that, when the master died, the animal guardian would contain his soul and carry it to the next experience. According to legend, when the cat died, then the master's soul was released to a heavenly destination.

Why such a feline is called a holy cat needs no explanation—but leap of faith? Well, it seems that the cat was enthroned next to the master, and when the master passed on while still sitting upright, the sacred cat leaped upon his head, and thus captured his soul. So doing, the Burmese cat changed from white to gold, and its eyes shifted from turquoise to sapphire. Too, the hundred cats of the temple transformed in the same way, all at the same time.

A lovely tale—yet here it comes again across the roundness of the ever changing, never changing void. This time, it comes in the form of the jumping cats of Phe Chaung monastery. These are resident cats that have been trained to jump through a series of hoops, "as a way of dealing with boredom," according to one article. We think not. No one, or thing, is ever bored in the Buddhist orientation of life. Nor would the monks have to "train" their cats, for, if the legend is true, the cats have leaps of faith encoded in their genes.

How different are these leaps from the little lion dogs turning prayer wheels in the Tibetan monasteries? Both the Tibetan spaniel and the Lhasa apso have the duty of rotating the prayer wheels of the monks. They are also great guard dogs, and their virtues have been praised over those of the mastiff.

The monastery cats that perform hoop-leaps aren't so dissimilar. They, too, were originally bred as monastic guardians, watching over grain, rice, and master alike.

Furthermore, the symbol of the hoop and the wheel are equals, too. Each represents the wheel of life, whereon—until we achieve salvation through enlightenment—we are wedded to the eternal life-and-death of the fleshly home.

Cats, more than dogs we think, are great meditators. Sitting upright, or lying sphinx-like with folded paw, they contemplate . . . what? Your guess is as good as ours, but time-honored myths associate cat eyes with lunar cycles and cat mind with the cosmos.

In Europe, too, the immovable, meditational cat was viewed as beneficial. Because she was both useful and quiet, this was the one animal permitted in the convent. According to the English Nun's Rule of 1205: "Dear Sisters, you must keep no beast other than a cat."

As well as leapers, changers, fixers of the unfixable universe, cats are also walkers, slouchers, lazers, and loungers. In undoing, in not doing, they regard the whirling traceries of life, and grimace silently unto themselves. However, when called upon to act, nothing moves more swiftly, more arrowlike to its goal, than a cat on the run.

Yet what about walking? We think of the great predatory cats as preternatural walkers and stalkers . . . how about domestic felines?

Once again, as hundreds of recent reports bear witness, cats will travel almost any distance to find their homes, their families. Whether you call it psi trailing or something else is irrelevant. Who cares what it was that motivated the newsworthy puss, Sugar, to walk fifteen hundred miles from California to Oklahoma to find his heart's Mecca, his family?

Most impressive of these translocational tales is the news item on Checkers, whose hind legs were paralyzed and whose hind end was ingeniously strapped into a homemade wheelchair. Front paws churning, Checkers chuffed along for a distance of seventy-five miles in just nineteen days and nights to find his family. Averaging nearly four miles a day, Checkers came paddle-whacking down the roadside. Nothing stopped him; nothing deterred him from his destination.

Some psychics maintain that cats like Sugar and Checkers are not using anything in particular to orient themselves. What they are using, they say, is their own nature.

For us, as humans, psi trailing is startling. But what is it for a cat?

Perhaps a cat's time continuum is as unlike ours as science fiction is unlike everyday reality. The self-centered cat, who is always moving gracefully through the timeless void, may travel, in a sense, blind. Which is to say, with inner sight. Because we know so little of it, this circumambulation astounds us.

However, the cat probably isn't traveling to, or towards, anything, but rather it's moving steadily within a kind of interior grid, a loran of the universe, within its own mind. Such a concept takes the lost out of found, and the found out of lost.

It's a bit like saying, "My cat turned up the other day," which we often say when felines have been lost and then suddenly appear. "Turned up" is a little like saying "landed up," which cats also do when they fall through space. Perhaps, then, cats are doing this all the time: landing on their feet in a continually moving world. We, on the other hand, are fixed—not fluid entities, who, by force it would seem, move to "get somewhere." Cats are always there—whether leaping, lying, or loafing.

They're just *there*!

Thank God someone is, for we can learn from them.

Our master and mistress, the still, the stolid, the melting, moving, amazing, multiplying cat.

The Tao of Mau

Kit Kat likes yoga. She reclines on the patio with her body curled like a question mark. Her front paws perfectly line up with a margin in the floor, as if this line were law.

Is she really doing yoga? Well, that, we think, is where people learned to do it, by studying animals—particularly cats and dogs.

From cats one learns the best postures of relaxation. We may call it yoga if we wish, but it's far less complicated than exercise—as far as the cat's concerned. Cats get in and out of these fabulous, curious, pretzel positions at a moment's notice. It's not work for them, it's sleep!

Not so sleep inducing for a human being, however. On the other hand, why not try being a cat? Many cat poses are fun to get into and they feel wonderful afterwards. That may be one of the many reasons that cats indulge in them—extra rest, which is needed by an animal that expends great amounts of energy in quick, frenetic bursts.

The other morning we glimpsed a puff of beige. It was Kit Kat streaking across the yard and then hopping up five feet onto the flat three-inch top of a fence pole. There she perched, birdlike and beautiful, her tail hanging down like a vine.

She didn't move a muscle for quite some time. Was she waiting for a photographer to take her picture? Was she meditating? Hunting? Just being? Was she enjoying the little circle formed by her paws and her rear-end, her preposterous composition, her body trimmed down to the circumference of a beer can?

Whatever it was, she likes the little round landing field of the fence pole top, and she goes to it often—and with the same confident leap, land, and sit. She looks for all the world like a sculpture, or a soft brown outgrowth, a lichen, on the fence pole.

Gerald and his brother learned to do gymnastics and wrestling from their father, who was accomplished in both sports. Gerald's dad was always learning new holds, new feints and twists from the family cats. He encouraged his children to observe cats at play and cats engaged in combat, and just about anything they did of a physical nature, because it was not only pretty to watch, it was most instructive. The pattern of jump, pounce, kick, and retreat was repeated over and over by two or more felines, playing and wrestling at the same time. The game was serious and humorous.

When Gerald was teaching physical education at a preparatory school, he offered a Taoist activity called cat wrestling.

He taught students to "tumble into each other's space without banging heads, or hurting one another." It was a sport of leap and out-leap, jump, roll, turn, and retreat. Players lay on the mat, leaped up to their feet, and dived over their opponents—whose approaches were fast and from the opposite direction, exactly like cats. Or, more particularly, they were exactly like kittens playing on the living room rug. Points were accorded to the player who exhibited the best escapes, the fastest and easiest approaches, the most skillful engagement of the opponent.

Cat wrestling is an animal-based martial art stemming from Taoist masters whose practice of watching cats, herons, and snakes led them into trying the same standing, kicking, and striking styles. Children enjoy cat wrestling because it's friendly, totally nonviolent. In this respect, it's not unlike tai chi, aikido, or even capoeira, the Brazilian martial art, wherein the movements are a series of synchronized cartwheels, handsprings, and dive rolls.

In all of these endeavors, the artist frees himself of his limitations by allowing the aggressor to enter his space in any way he wishes. From this incoming energy, like the waiting cat, the player rises, rolls, turns, and even does headspins with feet asprawl, to ward off—but not to seriously injure—his opponent. Thus, the body commands what happens, not the mind—just the natural free-flowing rhythm of the unimpeded human form. The free-form spontaneity, the quick liquidity, are appealing to anyone interested in the inner dynamic of the martial arts.

For centuries, the Chinese and the Japanese have honored the cat in visual art, literature, and the martial arts. This includes meditation—standing, sitting, and moving. All three postures are common in cats and they usually reveal a relaxed nature. What animal is more serene in repose than the cat whose eyes are open, but whose body—even in movement— appears to be so fully at rest? The ears may move but the rest of the cat is motionless. The eyes seem to drink in the silence, and the cat's sleek physique utilizes it.

The Zen poet Gary Snyder once said, "All animals are in *samadhi* most of the time," meaning they are in a trance-like state even when they are doing things. They see in and out at the same time. And, as Snyder once wrote, "nothing is seen except that which is truly seen." The eye is honed to perfection, and thinking is not restricted to, but is expanded by, not-thinking or just plain seeing.

The astonishing thing about cats is this paradigm—their being appears to be a part of everything, a blend of all that is. Right now, for instance, Kit Kat is standing next to a wicker chair and she has conformed to the curve of the chair's leg, so that she seems such an integral and beautiful part of it. How does a cat achieve separateness in togetherness? And yet, Kit Kat stands out and blends in, whenever she wishes—hunting or just "killing time." It's her rapturous poise that fixes our attention—on top of fences, by wicker chairs, in the cleft of a Bahamian blind, out of the sun, and as flat as a wafer.

In the course of a single day, Kit Kat will sit atop a fence; look down at us from the roof with a seemingly disembodied head; curl up and sleep on a glass table beside a magazine so that she resembles a folded purse; stalk a rabbit in high grass and not be seen except for the prick of her dark ears in the sun; lie on her back and expose her white, soft tummy fur, asking—no, begging—to be rubbed there; and last but not least, staring at her reflection in a still pool without moving.

This morning she followed a heron with her eyes, then her body, moved dreamily, meltingly into the heron's world without wanting to stalk it, just to imitate it. Which, we must add, is what we do when we play games like cat wrestling, or when we meditate with eyes half-lidded, allowing the world to go fuzzy gold and soft gray and painterly green.

Is this what a cat sees when she isn't seeing anything? Is this the eye candy that cats feast upon? The world at one with itself? The world let go, so that it kind of idles away? Then the world of one thousand things ceases to be threatening, and eventually, if you look long enough, it ceases to be anything.

And that is when the cat sleeps.

Well, it can't hurt to imitate Her Highness now and then, nor to achieve a moment or two of sightful cat-seeing. Karel Capek caught this beautifully in his poem "She," which describes what he imagines cats think of human actions.

She

This is my person
she is very powerful
she eats a lot
she is all eating
she is not beautiful
she is furless
she washes with water
she miaows poorly
sometimes she purrs in her sleep
she has become my mistress
because she ate something magnificent

she takes into her paw
a sharp black paw
that she uses to engrave white leaves
she can't play in any other way
she sleeps at night
instead of day
she can't see in the dark
she has few delights
she doesn't dream of the hunt
she doesn't sing with love
at dusk, at dark
when everything is alive
with darkness
she sits head bowed
scratching
with that black claw
on the white leaves

I hear the soft rustling of the claw
she lets me outside
where I go again
into the night voices
that become me
like a garment of crickets
and sighs and whispers
and messages
I can't tell her about
because her paws
are full of unplayful leaves

The cat's yogic grace is in letting go so completely that every supple muscle is relaxed and slack. We have watched Kit Kat melt—go from solid to liquid—and if you were to pick her up, she'd be limp as a wet washcloth. (One of the things we love to do is pick her up and smell her tummy, which is always lightly scented of pine.)

How much we have to learn from the cat when it comes to the art of relaxation. We humans go about it too ardently, as if being at ease were another kind of job. Basically, the cat is just more in tune with herself. Man, caught between human and animal response, stands undecided in the firmament of an old paradigm—angel or devil, beauty or the beast? We are unfortunately at opposing sides of our own conflicting nature.

The feline has it all over us in the art of *being*, as we possibly may have it all over her in the art of *becoming*.

No doubt, the cat may always be a cat—and no less complex for all of that—but we will not always be merely human . . . or so we would like to think.

Is that what puts the tension in us? Is that what uncoils the tension from the cat?

As the Grand Master in *Chronicles of Tao* by Deng Ming-Dao says, "One seeks not to go the way of other men but rather to follow the cycles of nature. Only then can one know renewal and rejuvenation. Through returning and going forth, expansion and contraction, one knows infinity and perhaps immortality. For at that point, one is wholly integrated with the Tao. One gives undivided attention to its vital energy, responding with the utmost pliancy. Then one can become like a newborn infant."

Or, we might add, like a playful kitten.

The Lonesome Traveler

Some stray cats connect so vividly and so readily that we cannot imagine what life would be like without them. And then, quixotic creatures that they are, one day they disappear.

Where do they go?

We don't know.

What do they do?

We haven't a clue.

Wayfarer cats are dropouts who just like to drop in. They are lonesome cats who stay for a time, leave for a time, and come back when it suits them—a year, two years . . . as in the strange case of our Siamese cat, Sammie. She stayed with us, off and on, for about twenty years. During which time she never spent more than a few days with us before she'd go off on one of her arcane errands.

We suspected, somehow, that Sammie had numerous homes, and that she made the rounds to each, for perhaps a few days or a few weeks at a time. Sammie was a midnight Siamese—black, silky, and smooth. We lived fourteen miles outside of town, but she turned up one day as if she'd always been there with us. She seemed to recognize us, even if we didn't know her. In any event, we let her run the household with an authority and familiarity that was acceptable to everyone except a few of our dogs, who quite naturally resented the intrusion.

So that was it. Sammie showed up, moved in, and took over all at the same time. We shrugged, wondering if she were a reincarnated person we had once known, because she had a omniscience about the whole thing that was very puzzling—she knew our every move better than we did.

The night Sammie appeared, there was some barking outside in the driveway as a big black Newfoundland showed up. He was a walking forest of burrs, tumors, cuts, and gouges. Worst of all, the poor dog had a split tongue, and was bleeding so profusely from the mouth we didn't think there was any hope of stopping it. Any animal lover knows that tongue-cuts do not heal quickly, if they heal at all. However, we got him to the vet who explained the Newf's prognosis was fair, all things considered. In time, he was healed of all his injuries.

So, a black cat and a black dog to match—bookends.

Over the next six months we enjoyed them both. They appeared to be great friends. Often, they went on walks together on the ridge above our house—the thunder-tailed, slow-footed black dog and the dainty-footed but unerring, high-tailed black cat. After that first six months, Sammie started disappearing on a regular basis. That left Black Dog disconsolate and alone. But Sammie always came back, and each time, she brought more vagabonds.

One time she brought in a magpie. It flew in through the open upper-story window the same morning Sammie returned. The bird woke us up, in fact, by pecking us gently on the lips. We put it outside and it stayed, building a nest and rearing a family a few feet from the house. The newborn magpies had a thin wail that was not unlike Sammie's mew, a strange coincidence, so that if she were gone, we imagined we heard her crying at the door.

Some time after this, Sammie brought home a tawny dog. He, like Black Dog and the magpie, seemed to know us from way back, but he was on a tight schedule and just stayed for a few weeks. Nonetheless, he came back frequently for a number of years.

Usually when Sammie came back, she looked quite underfed, as if she'd been on a long and perilous journey. We always spread a feast for her, wondering what creatures would come in her wake. We were never long in waiting. One time she brought a human with her. He was an odd little ragamuffin, part goblin and part man, who got stuck in our remote country driveway—it was a mile and a quarter of mud in the wintertime—and he came sloshing up to our front door with Sammie.

This funny little fellow acted like he'd known us for ages. He traded some very beautiful Pueblo pottery for a tow out of the mud, but he only stayed one night, telling us his gypsy tale of road-wearying adventures. He was a flea market man, traveling to open-air bazaars all over the Southwest, and his life was blissful but for one thing: he had rheumatoid arthritis.

When he left very early the next morning, he gave us (not part of the tow-trade) a black-incised Pueblo pot with a snake twined all around it. We still have it sitting in our living room, reminding us of Sammie and her strange assortment of picaresque pals.

Then Sammie went away and didn't come back for almost a year. On her return visit, she sauntered in mewing madly and was fatter than we'd ever seen her. Two days later, Sammie had kittens. She deposited them in the closet, and, just like that, she was gone again! From this amazing litter came two of our favorite felines, Moonie and Tigger.

Moonie was Siamese and Tigger was tabby. They each stayed with us for the rest of their lives, and they never strayed once.

One morning, about ten years after Sammie first came to see us, we were startled to see that she had begun to look feeble. Her visits got longer and longer until, at last, she showed no inclination to leave. She was always an affectionate cat, but now she showered us with affection. Her constant, illimitable purring filled the house with music. Wherever we were, there she was—singing. At night she climbed on our bed and "made bread" and licked the insides of our ears. She stayed indoors, not going out for six months, during which time she never left our sight.

Then, one bright morning, she wasn't anywhere to be seen. The saddest thing was her missing purr. No more purring Sammie. We looked everywhere— she was nowhere to be found. She'd gone again—and this time, we knew it was for good.

She didn't come back, nor did we have any more peculiar visits from her friends. Black Dog was old and crippled, but he stayed with us a few more years. The bright magpies of the morning made more nests in our aspen trees, and in the spring, the crying of the babies always reminded us of Sammie, which was a great comfort. But the old homestead seemed so lonely, so abandoned without that come-and-go cat. We were looking out for her, hoping she'd come up the driveway, tail extended and mewing hoarsely, but it never happened.

That was not the end of Sammie, however—not by a long shot.

Our door was open, and she knew it. Wherever she was, whatever lovely essence she'd become, she was out there in the cosmos somewhere, waiting for her release papers. One morning, the front door unlatched and creaked open. It opened wide. Nothing was there. This happened a number of times. Once we said in unison, as the door creaked open, admitting a sunlit wind, "Sammie, is that you?" But it was only the autumn air, and nothing we could see.

Then one night Gerald dreamed about a stark, dead leafless tree. Underneath, there was a man with a box of puppies. Gerald woke up, and for the rest of the day he was haunted by this dream. The following day, he and our daughter Hannah took a drive to a nearby town where they had a picnic lunch at the local park. There on the green was a bent old apple tree, and under it, a man with a wooden box. A sign in front of the box said, "free puppies." Gerald and Hannah selected a round, fuzzy ball that grunted incessantly and cried only once as they took it home.

On the drive back, they talked about the dream-like quality of the day, the beauty of the sunset, the gold glow of the autumn trees, the cuteness of the puppy in the back seat, and the wonderful and mysterious way things happen when you embrace your dreams and honor them.

That pup was named Mocha and she grew to be a fine and lovely Akita dog, a worthy friend of Sammie, who, even though she wasn't there proved she was always there, drawing us into new relationships, and always finding homes for lost dogs, and reminding us that cat magic is not to be taken for granted. Sammie's still there and we never will find out who she was, or is, or will be again. Like the playwright William Saroyan once said, "the tiger . . . is love."

The Cherub and the Tiger

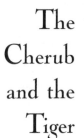

The cat is perfection in action—an angelic tiger. So, what happens when this paragon of beauty uses the shower as a cat box?

When told in no uncertain terms that this wasn't the place to go, the goddess cat looks up, as if to say, "*Mais oui*, but where would you have me go?"

Whereupon we say, "Try using the toilet, as we do."

Thereafter, the cat does what we have asked, uses the toilet. One particularly enlightened cat belonging to our mother actually learned how to flush. (Mostly, though, as cat lovers know, the whole action of disposal by water is without aesthetic value to a cat. Kit

Kat values her outdoor catbox of pine-scented sand, and she revisits her leavings from time to time because these are marked places on the property, which make the standard flush a complete waste of useful cat waste, so to speak.)

Cats are so much smarter than human beings allow them to be in the standard contract of cat-at-home. Given the right inducement, the proper opportunity, and the most obliging and patient human, a domestic cat can do almost anything. That's what the myth of Puss in Boots is about, incidentally. The contract should read: If the cat's so inclined, it shall be able to do, or undo, anything.

But the thing is, said cat *must* be so inclined; otherwise it shall do nothing.

Essentially, cats do *only* what *they* want to do, and that too is conditional—meaning, *when* they want to do it. The rest of the time, they befuddle us with their superior indifference and their seemingly abysmal ignorance of our affairs.

The upshot of this in most households is a well-chilled cat that travels on its own course. Well, as a general rule, we let cats that let us alone *even more* alone—hence, they gain their freedom by pretending to ignore us. But don't be fooled, it's just a trick—they're watching all the time.

Within a split second, the sleepy tabby can blossom into a tigery wonder. All we have to do, it seems, is to really want this to happen, to be ready for it to happen, and to sort-of midwife it into being.

Goddess cats. We've all known a few. You know, they're the ones who travel thousands of miles on three legs to be reunited with their friends. They're the ones who, like Sammie, know no bounds, who come and go and visit worlds beyond our knowledge, and return with the glimmer of distance in their eyes (perhaps it's not worlds but dimensions they're visiting).

Charles Perrault's Puss in Boots is a male cat that comes from a female tradition of cat winners—he's actually the mistress of the corn motif, the sacred grain cat. Male or female, this is the harvest puss. The super mouser. The cat whose spirit, once given to the earth, enshrines the corn, the wheat, the barley, the grain, and enriches our lives just by touching them. (Sammie did this, by the way. For, whenever she was around we had good luck).

Historically, as European culture got away from agrarian pursuits, the cat got a whole new identity, and one that has stuck to the present time. This incarnation is rather inglorious but quite safe: Ms. Kitty. Plain old house pet.

However, in myth, the cat's magnificence remains, still untarnished. Deep down, Puss in Boots, that cavalier cat of fortune, is still alive. Like the genie in the lamp, we imagine a good rubbing might bring the old electricity—and so it does, literally speaking anyway, whenever you pet a cat's fur.

The truth is, we still hold onto the magical cat, the angel tiger, and—you may laugh at this, but the patron saint of lawyers and virgins is still the cat. It's a little difficult to equate the two professions—unless you consider that a hard truth or a rigid lie can easily spoil them—but this was, and still is, the saint cat of Italy, an angel tiger of the courts and beds.

We've seen something of the angel tiger ourselves . . . with a little help from Gerald's mom, Mimi. When this mystic woman was in her mid-eighties, she began to have hallucinations. One recurring theme was of a tiny tiger that burned bright in the forests of the night just beyond her bedroom window. This tiger was accompanied by a flute boy, a kind of Kokopelli, who charmed her with his enchanting melodies. In the garden of real rhododendrons, the tiger shone in the dark leaves.

Try though we might, we never saw him.

Mimi asked, "Can't you see the tiger?"

It exasperated her that we couldn't see the flame-patterned feline that so delighted her eye. From a psychological point of view, the tiger represented love and balance in the unstable world of aging and loneliness. Some time after Mimi passed on, we asked our daughter, who was often with Mimi when the little tiger appeared if she could see the tiger.

"No," she answered, "but I've wished that I had seen him. Nothing would've given me more joy than to see that angel cat the way Mimi saw him in the night, lighting up the leaves."

Angel-winged, the tiger cometh, whispering softly of death and transfiguration. In China, the tiger is a living symbol of beauty and cruelty. He is the new moon and the darkness. In India, he is the force of chaos, but in Europe he is the beast that rages in the human heart.

The English poet, William Blake, recognized the angel tiger as a beast of duality, and he raised a riddle for all to see: Did He who made the Lamb make thee?

The riddle is as old as time. Predating it is the famous koan: "If a man hangs by a root over the edge of a cliff and a hungry tiger paces grimly below, what shall the man do . . . let go, or seek to pull himself up, thereby snapping the root and plunging himself to his fate?"

The koan has remained throughout the centuries as a human paradox which can't be cracked. For the tiger is either full of love or blind with hate. Which tiger do you choose as you fall?

A Tale
of Two
Misanthropes

Sometimes you get the feeling, the sneaking suspicion, so to say—that some cats are really not fond
of people; or worse, they actually *like* to *dislike*
humans. John Steinbeck, when he visited Eleanor
Brace on Deer Isle, Maine, met her housecat George,
a misanthropic coon cat. The author brought along
his pet poodle, Charley. You may remember that
Charley was the amiable and irascible star of
Steinbeck's classic memoir *Travels with Charley.*

Anyway, this is the cat episode he recounted.

That was George. He didn't welcome me and he didn't particularly welcome Charley. I never did rightly see George, but his sulking presence was everywhere. For George is an old gray cat who has accumulated a hatred of people and things so intense that even hidden upstairs he communicates his prayer that you will go away. If the bomb should fall and wipe out every living thing except Miss Brace, George would be happy. That's the way he would design a world if it were up to him. And he could never know that Charley's interest in him was purely courteous; if he did, he would be hurt in his misanthropy, for Charley has no interest in cats whatever, even for chasing purposes.

One wonders if there aren't some bestirred gene pool arguments in this bit of fur and fluff. For instance, Marie Antoinette was supposed to have given the Marquis de Lafayette a couple of Angora cats (the first Middle Eastern-bred cats brought to America) for a present. Sent by ship in the 1700s, they supposedly got lost or redirected, somehow ending up as a breed in the islands of Maine.

We shall never know if this tidbit is true. And we may also wonder if Charley, being of purer and more refined French genes, sensed George was a backwoods ruffian and thus looked down his historical nose at him. Or was it, as Steinbeck suggested, the reverse? George's xenophobia was so finely tuned that this cat was a grayish cloud of misanthropy from the get-go. Like some people we know, he couldn't abide the idea of a dog, even as a joke.

Some cats, most cats, are like that, especially when left to their own devices. And George certainly had been left to his.

Deer Isle is a perfect place to be stranded—if you are a poet, a misanthropic poet, a reclusive coon cat, or perhaps just a weekend or a summer visitor. However, we've been there, and we've met some *lifers*—cats who stayed on for generations. Maybe these were the original gift cats of Ms. Antoinette, but at any rate, we found them eccentric and fascinating, not to mention cute, and we took one home with us.

That cat developed a baleful glare and an inclination to abide in attics. She, like George, wished the world would go away. And there was no talking her out of it. She vanished like smoke the moment a car came up the drive. On occasion, for no apparent reason, she attacked circumspect and reasonable strangers. Her front feet were of the traditional seventoed variety, and when she flailed them, she could do serious damage to human flesh.

Some years after acquiring the coon cat, our brother got a Persian that resembled her. This feline, too, prayed you'd go away as soon as you arrived at her doorstep. She walked wispily, as if the floor were made of moss and she were all feints and fades and nothing so substantial as fur and bone.

Well, one day we made the mistake of picking her up. She shrieked and yowled and soared into the air, and dashed vertically across the wall and then disappeared into the next room. The lesson, if there is one: Do not look a misanthrope in the eye . . . ?

Normal cats—that is to say, cats without curmudgeonly responses to normal situations—don't mind being picked up, usually. But what cat likes to be suddenly brought face-to-face with a human? Even the most genial feline will object to the rush and may scratch to get away from such proximity. Kit Kat, who tends to be very friendly with us most of the time, will often purr when we pick her up. But she's always warding the face away with a cold-padded paw. This is frequently pressed upon the jaw of the offending face. Her China-blue eyes, unblinking at first, soon close as if the violation of personal space is more than she can bear . . . and rightly so, we think.

The concept of personal space seems to have been designed by felines. Coming from different quarters on the tree of life, we learned it from them: the idea that one mustn't share facial space. We once faced a bobcat in this way and got a bit more than we bargained for.

After a few minutes of idle unblink, the cat's face seemed to change, the facial stripes got darker. The gold eyes closed, as if the confined cat were wishing itself light-years away. Then it stood up and stretched, and its bobbed tail trembled and its claws sprouted. The cat yawned pink and pretty, and then dived at the screen in the door that separated us, and made our hearts stop with the suddenness of that leap.

Rule one, don't stare vehemently at cats—or any animal for that matter. You can often humble or humiliate an aggressive dog by doing this, but you ought to know what you are doing when you try it, for it can be dicey, especially when you don't know the dog.

Rule two, don't crowd or confine a cat.

Rule three, don't act as if you know a feline when you don't. Some cats take years to know, others take centuries. Some cats, as we've been saying right along, can't be known at all. They are utterly unknowable.

Some simple animal rules of conduct might be the following:

When working with animals of any kind, remember the size of your face versus the size of your eyes.

Our eyes, the seat of our soul, can be large or small, depending on makeup, eyeglasses, or merely emotional emphasis. Hats and heads figure largely in this, too. Our parrot George will attack anyone with "big hair," an unfamiliar hat, or something that extends or enlarges the shape of the human head.

Animals look to our heads and eyes to see what we are thinking and feeling. They study our hand movements with infinite interest, and our overall body language. Alarmed eyes—even those accented by makeup—may mean trouble to an animal. Fast-moving hands will always draw fire from George, who regards them as potential enemies as well as friendly places to perch.

Come to think of it, George is more misanthropic than his namesake in *Travels with Charley*, and he eyes all strangers with instant suspicion and disdain. When his pupils dilate, he is really measuring us. Gaiting, it's called with cats, this jiggling and sighting thing that they do with their eyes. When George does it, beware. He's sizing you up. If he doesn't like what he sees, he'll fly at your face, claws outstretched.

George, like some cats we know, is an uncertain quantity most of the time. Very surprising things come out of his beak, too. Like the time he saw our dachshund, Beeper, have a diarrhea attack on the floor. "Poor thing," he said in a commiserative tone. Or the time an artist friend of ours dropped by unexpectedly, and George, pacing to and fro on his perch, said in a cranky voice, "Too busy to talk to you now." The funniest repartee of George's came after Gerald had concluded a phone call with a difficult agent, sighed and said, "What an asshole." Whereupon George replied unhesitatingly, "You're the asshole." George says what he means, and he means what he says. And he is an unstinting truth-sayer.

But back to cats: We know one who waited several years to attack a person that she didn't like. Then, one night, completely unprovoked, the cat slipped into our guest bedroom, jumped on our guest's face, and clawed him unmercifully. This guest, by the way, had a bad habit of staring at the cat for long periods of time. We told him not to, but he did it anyway.

A friend told of a real tiger in Burma that came out of the jungle and walked into a tent where he was sleeping. The tiger stood by his cot staring at his closed eyes. Our friend feigned sleep for quite a long time. The tiger finally went away. What if our friend had awakened and opened his eyes wide? All of this eye-chat, however, comes round at last to another catty conundrum. Are domestic cats nothing less than smaller versions of their larger, predatory relations?

Are there some *Felidae* who are more mink than panther? More fox than tiger?

Is the ancient myth of the tabby who came in from the cold true? Is this cat who forsook his best friend, Tiger, for the warmth of a human hearth real?

Are cats cold-blooded killers whose instincts allow them to enjoy the macabre pact between cat and mouse that goes, "Run and I will find you . . . hide and I will seek you . . . and when I find you, I will torture you"?

Is this what makes cats misanthropes in the company of humans? They could do the same to us at any time—in their minds, anyway, if only we were the size of a mouse. Some cats must wish this fate upon us as well. How about when we hold them too tightly and smother them with kisses? They know we wouldn't dare if they were a little larger.

The theme is nicely summed up by Matthew Arnold in "Poor Matthias."

> Down she sank amid her fur;
> Eyed thee with a soul resign'd—
> And thou deemedst cats were kind!
> —Cruel, but composed and bland,
> Dumb, inscrutable and grand,
> So Tiberius might have sat,
> Had Tiberius been a cat.

Various writers over the centuries have ventured the opinion that cats have an edge on people. Cats don't need to know us in order to have the complete dossier. All the cat has to do is read our minds.

Amy Rapaport, senior editor at *Vegetarian Times*, says this about her character-wise cat, Toby, who sees All and knows All:

"A few years after my divorce, I got into a bad relationship with a guy Toby hated. Stupid me, I moved in with him, and from that moment until the day I moved out, I watched my cat's health deteriorate right before my eyes. Toby never came out from under the bed, he hissed and scratched whenever the guy got near him, and he stopped eating. I was sure he was dying. . . . Yet the very day I packed my stuff into my car and drove away with Toby in the backseat, he sprang back to life—happy, healthy, and my friend again."

So often cats express the inexpressible—the very things we think about unconsciously. We have known our share of fast-study felines and quick-opinion humans, and all things considered, they are a lot alike. However, the silent telepathic cat can't be won over. An opinion formed by such an omniscient cat is indelible. As they say, the leopard's spots don't wash out.

Who
Hates
Cats,
and
Why?

Cat haters—*ailurophobes*, what of them?

Are they the same people who were largely and collectively responsible for the mass feline murders of the Middle Ages?

Are they, symbolically speaking, the children who tied firecrackers to cat's tails? The same ones who tossed the kitty out the attic window to see if she'd land on all fours?

And, what about the lop-headed men who decided long ago that cats were witches?

No, we're talking about people whom you know, who have a potent grudge against cats—but not a grudge that is inflicted or imposed upon the cat—these are just folks who don't like them. Once again, we think of Aunt Glad, who adored animals, even snakes and lizards, but she couldn't abide cats—"Creeping cats give me the creeps." Yet she had a special place in her heart for dogs and birds. Many ailurophobes are like that. They love dogs and positively hate cats, and they act as if there were no choice in the matter.

Why has the cat been so cruelly misrepresented, so disastrously mistreated by humans over the past two to three thousand years? In fact, only snakes have been treated worse, which makes us wonder if the serpent/cat configuration, dating back to ancient Egypt, might explain the revulsion. Both cats and snakes are silent assassins and the cat has been dubbed the "furred serpent."

Or is it—the hating business, we mean—merely the other side of the two-sided coin? Cat goddess on one side, sorceress on the other. The fact is, people who abhor cats get visibly ill when the feline name is mentioned. Asthmatics who loathe cat fur get teary-eyed and wheezy at the sight of a cat. Well, the word *ailuros* in Greek means "waving ones" and it refers to ship cats brought aboard to kill mice. However, linguists also tell us that *ailuros* may refer to the snowy-breasted martens. So, go figure.

The most famous ailurophobe in history was apparently Napoleon. According to popular legend, he was once discovered in his palace doing swordplay with the shadow of a cat cast upon a tapestry. Reportedly, the greatest military mind of his time had violent nightsweats over the presence of a puss.

Carl Van Vechten (*The Tiger in the House*) says, "No, it is not from people who fear cats that puss's greatest enemies are recruited. Perhaps unjust and stupid historians have had something to do with the occasional disfavor in which domestic felines are held."

His comments point to the thing that all cat lovers have heard a million times before: "Cats are as faithless as dogs are faithful." However, we would like to know where cats got this undue reputation for fickle friendship, for in truth, there is nothing more steadfast than a cat. Cats stick unnaturally close to their chosen ones.

You've heard the old saw that cats aren't heroic, but dogs are courageous and loyal unto death. Well, once again, the faith of the cat and her hero's heart ought not to be questioned. Puss in Boots is a good example of this and so are some of the tales by the Brothers Grimm where the cat so cleverly saves the day, the night, the simpleton, and the prince.

In the Grimm tale, "The Poor Miller's Boy and the Little Cat," a kindly, yet simpleminded apprentice youth, who is not expected to inherit his master's mill because he cannot not live up to the miller's request of bringing home a very fine horse, meets up with a charmed, speckled cat.

She took him to her bewitched little palace where she had nothing but cats to wait on her. They leaped nimbly up and down the stairs, happy and full of fun. In the evening, when they sat down to supper, there were three who made music; one played the double bass, another the violin, and the third put the trumpet to her mouth and blew up her cheeks for all she was worth. When they had eaten, the table was removed and the cat said, "Come, John, dance with me." "No," said he, "I don't dance with pussycats. That's something I have never done."

John learns, however, to appreciate cats. He learns their ways and wiles and becomes a kind of man-in-training. He passes seven years with the cats and is essentially a servant to them, while they, in turn, also serve him. This paradigm is much like a good marriage, wherein there is harmony and balance in the roles of both male and female partners. The cats in the Grimm tale are all female, while John is a kind of nonsexed or undefined male figure. As he matures in cat wisdom, he is given a magnificent horse, but more importantly, the speckled cat turns into a lovely princess, who marries him and confers great wealth upon him. Also, he inherits the mill.

The innocence of the tale is implicit, but it is also a portrait of a time in Europe when good old cat magic was yet in force. A man in the story must serve as well as be served.

For those of whom cats are most fond, they give everything they have, including their lives. Cats like the famous Scarlet, who saved her kittens in a burning building, also rescue humans as often as their own kin. Cats can be most sacrificing and unselfish, and are far from the stereotype of the self-serving feline.

Some say it's the psychic nature of the feline that offends many of the male persuasion. And, as women are thought to have this extra defense as well, cats and women have been given a bad reputation for being . . . well, protective, among other things.

Ambrose Bierce defines the cat in his famous dictionary as, "A soft indestructible automaton provided by nature to be kicked when things go wrong in the domestic circle." This cuts close to the truth, as women do not, as a rule, "kick the cat," but it is the habit, mythologically speaking, of frustrated men—and frequently men frustrated only by women.

If one analyzes Bierce's jeweled phrase, a lot of wisdom is derived from it. Such words as "indestructible automaton" and "domestic circle" seem, in a way, to exclude male participation. Since the cat is very often the historical companion of women, and since men would like to be thought of as indestructible, it's not difficult to see why a male prejudice could arise here. In addition, the cat is said to be and is "soft," as men are *not*, psychically as well as physically.

The Bierce words with the most power are "domestic circle." The man, often enough, stands outside this familial, female roundness. Which is to say, he may be the *first* to go. Not Puss, who as proverb tells us, comes back the very next day.

Therefore, an irritated man's only recourse is to kick the cat, which he has done, historically, going back to the beginning.

The domestic cat has also been labeled deceitful, cunning, and crafty. At its worst, the cat's been called "in league with the Devil," but we've already gone into that. Naturally, cats are crafty and they have *had* to be cunning—how else to survive in a world set against them? Even the famous Dr. Samuel Johnson said of the cat: "A domestick animal that catches mice, commonly reckoned by naturalists the lowest order of the leonine species."

So, when historians weren't enjoying cat-bashing, naturalists and authors were at home doing it. Once more, the important words in Dr. Johnson's presentation are *domestick* and *lowest order*. This would define the eighteenth century character of women. Men are outside of the domestic circle of fecundity, birthing, and home-making. In this respect, perhaps, they, the men, are the lowest order.

Why do men in myths hate the cat? Arguably, because of this inner circle of secret sensitivity: the troika of cat/witch/broom. Therefore, in men's eyes, the woman was the midwife of magic. Her broom was a pestle for crushing potions, as well as a phallic symbol—which signifies a woman-minus-man scenario.

By calling a feline "the lowest order of the leonine species," Dr. Johnson redefined his own prejudices. Ailurophobes all, each and every one, all those men who mentally kick the cat. "Touch not the cat" is the old phrase, and it is likely a protective omen, a blessing. For it wasn't really the cat that women were trying to save, but themselves.

The abuse from cat haters was just another kind of misogyny.

However, let's not miss the issue, or mistreat men, or get generally out of line in our reasoning. What we're really talking about is a cultural phenomenon that exists, and has existed in large measure, in Europe, the British Isles, and America.

It is not as true in the Middle East, where Mohammed cut off his sleeve so he wouldn't waken his slumbering cat when he went to say his prayers. Nor in Asia, where the cat advised the emperors and bore them to Heaven; nor in the Mediterranean, where magical cats brought riches to commoners as often as common cats brought rich manners to the kings and queens.

No, the curse on cats has come mainly from "our part of the world." Hillaire Belloc, the French poet, seemed to say it all for the men of Europe when he remarked that cats ". . . will drink beer. This is not a theory; I know it; I have seen it with my own eyes."

Well, any creature that has the temerity—and the tenacity—to drink a man's beer without his permission, we of course assume, is to be despised. Or to be very closely watched.

Case closed.

Cats beware.

The war against your species still twinkles malevolently under the sleepy surface of the collective human memory, as evidenced by this old English nursery rhyme.

I love little puss
Her coat is so warm;
And if I don't hurt her
She'll do me no harm.

Unless, of course, you believe—
as we do—that cats are catalysts, if
you will, for dogs, human and otherwise, to be
scurrilous dogs.

Smart's Cat

The eighteenth century poet, Christopher Smart, while confined to an asylum for the insane, wrote the unfinished collection of verse, *Jubilate Agno*, and in it we find several lines to "my cat Jeoffrey," which represent one of the world's greatest cat poems.

Some believe Smart's poem is the finest "feline writing" in English literature. A tall order? Well, he sees himself and his cat as confined to a jail—physical and spiritual—and it's through this that he envisions a cat's (and a human's) world. Incarcerated, the two, Christopher and Jeoffrey, are free to see what they will and to imagine what they might. And while examining Jeoffrey's joyous behavior, poet Smart delves deeply into the psyche of the feline and into the religion of humans.

In this way, Smart's cat becomes the doorway to enlightenment, the window unto God's face.

No doubt, Christopher was thinking of himself when his admiration of the feline spilled over into rapture. He was saying, in effect, that "My cat and I are one, and oneness *is* godliness."

If Blake's "tyger" is the malevolent dark side of the feline equation, Smart's madcap Jeoffrey is the antic, upbeat, bright side. For Smart sees only configurations of bliss in his cat's sinews and soul. Furthermore, even Jeoffrey's predatory nature is excused, as it were, "for the dexterity of his defense is an instance of the love of God to him exceedingly."

In his ablutions and his acrobatics, Jeoffrey proves his godliness, his attractiveness to his maker—so says Smart, many times over. And, in so saying, the poet reveals that all things have their beauty in God's eyes, but in few is the cat equaled for "the variety of his movements" and "God's light" about him, his ability to "tread to all the measures upon the musick."

The latter phrase refers to what we would call feline grace, but also to that which is humanly untouchable in the cat—its unique inspirational and religious context. For, as Smart reminds us, the cat is "good to think on" and he warns us *not* to be like the cat, but that we, in our daily lives, should try to express ourselves just as neatly. It's amazing how much morality Christopher Smart finds in his cell-mate, how much aphorism and metaphor, the sum of which is a kind of feline Bible—"For he counteracts the powers of darkness by his electrical skin and glaring eyes. / For he counteracts the Devil, who is death, by brisking about the life."

Life, says Smart, is godly. And the cat—his cat, Jeoffrey—is the most goodly, godly example of this in the universe . . . and why not? Smart's physical universe is quite small, but while he contemplates Jeoffrey, it expands into infinity.

Jeoffrey can "swim for life . . . can creep," "can jump from an eminence into his master's bosom." He can, therefore, outleap the confines of his physical prison-body, and break free into the spiritual domain of Heaven. He is not, as such, jailed. He is not in a madhouse, dying of boredom. He is not sentenced but unsentenced; free to go about as he will, this mir-acle achieved by exercise of will.

Smart even admits that Jeoffrey "knows that God is his savior" and that "there is nothing sweeter than his peace when at rest." Clean conscience, ultimate peace with the Creator, who could want more?

Christopher Smart's classic poem ensured that its author, who was considered insane, should always be remembered for his poetic genius. According to Fernand Mery (*The Life, History and Magic of the Cat*), Smart's lines "share the quality of imaginative madness—and a feeling for feline mystery—with William Blake." However, Smart's electrical cat can leap beyond human thought, his cat is tenacious of spirit, devout, and humble and "the instrument for children to learn benevolence upon." In short, this is not the same animal pictured by Blake, who couldn't figure out the Maker's riddle—"What immortal hand or eye / Could frame thy fearful symmetry?" Smart's cat is cute; Smart's smart cat is love. An antidote to the ailurophobe's remark, "The cat and man are unified in their ability to kill cleverly and without compassion."

Smart replies—"For when he takes his prey he plays with it to give it a chance." And, indeed, he prefigures Darwin when he adds, "For one mouse in seven escapes by his dallying."

Blake offers no such consolation in "The Tyger." In fact, Blake says that if the lamb is the creation of God, what was the Creator thinking when he made the tiger? He mollifies us with the beautiful symmetry of the tiger's design, implying that beauty is its own answer to the unanswerable koan, *Why?*

We who love Puss have our own secret, heartfelt answer to the cat conundrum, but none of us have perhaps put it so intently and so religiously as Christopher Smart. Here is the excerpt from Smart's *Jubilate Agno*.

For Jeoffrey

For I will consider my cat Jeoffrey.

For he is the servant of the living God, duly and daily serving him.

For at the first glance of the glory of God in the East he worships in his way.

For this is done by wreathing his body seven times round with elegant quickness.

For when he leaps up to catch the musk, which is the blessing of God upon his prayer.

For he rolls upon prank to work it in.

For having done duty and received blessing he begins to consider himself.

For this he performs in ten degrees.

For first he looks upon his forepaws to see if they are clean.

For secondly he kicks up behind to clear away there.

For thirdly he works it upon stretch with the forepaws extended.

For fourthly he sharpens his paws by wood.

For fifthly he washes himself.

For sixthly he rolls upon wash.

For seventhly he fleas himself, that he be not interrupted upon the beat.

For eighthly he rubs himself against a post.

For ninthly he looks up for his instructions.

For tenthly he goes in quest of food.

For having considered God and himself he will consider his neighbor.

For if he meets another cat he will kiss her in kindness.

For when he takes his prey he plays with it to give it chance.

For one mouse in seven escapes by his dallying.

For when his day's work is done his business more properly begins.

For he keeps the Lord's watch in the night against the adversary.

For he counteracts the powers of darkness by his electrical skin and glaring eyes.

For he counteracts the devil, who is death, by brisking about the light.

For in his morning orisons he loves the sun and the sun loves him.

For he is of the tribe of tiger.

For the Cherub Cat is a term of the Angel Tiger.

For he has the subtlety and hissing of a serpent, which in goodness he suppresses.

For he will do destruction, if he is well fed, neither will he spit without provocation.

For he purrs in thankfulness, when God tells him he's a good Cat.

For he is an instrument for the children to learn benevolence upon.

For every house is incomplete without him and a blessing is lacking in spirit . . .

For the English cats are the best in Europe.

For he is the cleanest in use of his forepaws of any quadrupeds.

For the dexterity of his defense is an instance of the love of God to him exceedingly.

For he is quickest to his mark of any creature.

For he is tenacious of his point.

For he is a mixture of gravity and waggery.

For he knows that God is the Savior.

For there is nothing sweeter than his peace when at rest.

For there is nothing brisker than his life when in motion . . .

For he is docile and can learn certain things . . .

For he can jump from an eminence into his master's bosom.

For he can catch the cork and toss it again . . .

For he is good to think on, if a man would express himself neatly . . .

For by stroking of him I have found out electricity.

For I perceive God's light about him both wax and fire.

For the Electrical fire is the spiritual substance, which God sends from heaven to sustain the bodies both of man and beast.

For God has blessed him in the variety of his movements.

For, though he cannot fly, he is an excellent clamberer.

For his motions upon the face of the earth are more than other quadrupeds.

For he can tread to all the measures upon the musick.
For he can swim for life.
For he can creep.

And Leopard Said . . .

For those who wish to go back farther than Smart, Blake, or the Bible; back to the beginning, back to firelight and dream, to the first origin myth of the feline, here then is the oldest myth we know that explains the ineffable nature of the cat, the tribe of tiger. . . .

Once there were gods who trod upon the Earth and called it home. There were gods in the heavens, too, and there were gods who moved swiftly upon the waters. It was a time of magic when magnificent beings appeared like flowers that bloom in a single day and are soon gone.

On such an occasion, a woman found an offering on her doorstep. She was a common person, nothing special. Nor had anything special ever happened to her.

"What is this?" she asked the gods of heaven, and she heard a voice that came out of the air.

"Here is something new," the voice said, "and something old."

On her doorstep was a kitten. Yet it was like no kitten on Earth because it was so perfectly, so divinely, made. Its fur was spider-spun silk and its ears, rose-petaled and pretty, were softer than air and as smooth as water.

"With such a lovely tail, you could paint the Dome of Heaven," the woman exclaimed.

She was overjoyed to have the cat, and she picked it up and kissed it. However, a thought came to her—"What if this treasure cat is not for me? I am a humble person. Surely this kitten belongs to someone great and important. And I must find out who that is."

So saying, she set off to find a being equal to the magnificence of the jewel-eyed kitten. Now, as the woman's bamboo house faced east and the rising Sun greeted her, she decided that the Sun should be offered the kitten. After all, wasn't the Sun the first presence of the day to touch her and the last presence to leave her? And didn't the Sun govern all who live by day? Certainly, the Sun was the proper one to whom the kitten should be offered.

The woman did not have to travel far either, for the Sun was everywhere.

"Sun," said the woman. "You are the greatest person in the world. Therefore, I offer you this wonderful kitten." And she raised the little cat into the abundance of beautiful sunshine.

The light listened. A voice was heard as the Sun spoke.

"What a perfect kitten," said the Sun. "And I should know because I put my light on all things. Still, I am not the greatest person in the world."

"Who is greater?" asked the woman.

And the Sun replied, "Rain, for when she lowers her veil, it is I who must hide."

The woman understood that there was something greater than the Sun, and, as she wondered when she might see Rain again, her question was answered. Just then, darkness came and covered the light of the Sun and the earth was wetted with raindrops.

"Rain," said the woman, "you have come at the right time, and as you are the greatest person in the world, I offer you this fine kitten."

Through the drops of water, the Rain softly spoke.

"I am honored," said the Rain, "for I see that, drop for drop, your gift is very fine, indeed. Yet there is someone greater than I to whom you should make this offering."

"Greater than you?" said the woman, astonished. "Who might that be?"

"Wind," said the Rain, "is greater because he chases me away whenever he wants."

The woman knew that what the Rain said was just and true, and she hastened to seek the Wind out. However, she did not look far, as a breath of warm air suddenly smote her cheek.

"Here, Wind," she gestured, raising the little cat into the generous breeze. "I give this wonderful kitten to you, for I know that you, above all, are the greatest there is."

The Wind whistled.

"Thank you for your wonderful gift," the Wind breathed. "But, I, the greatest? Surely, you know that there is one greater than I am?"

The woman shook her head in surprise.

"Who is greater than you?"

"Strong though I am, I cannot budge the tiniest anthill. No, I am no match for Ant."

The woman knew that what the Wind said was the truth. Away she went with the kitten. Finding a nearby anthill, she said, "Ant, as you are the greatest thing there is, please accept this precious gift."

In a moment, Ant appeared, carrying a leaf.

"I am not that great," Ant said humbly. Your gift is lovely, but I am not worthy of it, for there is one greater than I."

"Who is that?" the woman asked wearily.

"It is he who tramples my cities, reducing them to dust. The one I speak of is Bull."

The woman realized the wisdom of this, and she hastened now to find Bull, but she had not far to look. There under a flame-heart tree was Bull, at rest, indolently munching some grass.

"Here, Bull," she said presenting the little cat. "I give you, the greatest one there is, this precious kitten."

The Bull meditated solemnly on the gift. Then he shook his huge, curved horns, and spoke deeply and wisely.

"I cannot accept your kindness. I should like to, but there is one greater than I."

"Who could possibly be your better?" the woman wanted to know.

And Bull replied tersely, "Leopard."

Now the woman knew that Leopard took whatever she wished, whenever she wanted to, and therefore Bull was telling the truth. She left Bull where he rested in the shade and sought the spotted shape of the tree-dwelling Leopard.

When she found her, stretched out on a huge, twisted acacia branch, she sighed, respectfully, "Leopard, since it is known that you are the greatest, I have come to make you an offering."

Leopard blinked. She was not pleased at the disturbance; she valued her time of rest and did not enjoy visitations.

"Who told you that I was the greatest?" she rumbled down deep in her throat.

The woman explained, "I visited the Sun, who told me he was not greater than the Rain, who told me she was not greater than the Wind, who told me that he was not greater than the Ant, who told me that she was not greater than Bull, who told me that he was not greater than you; therefore, you are the greatest, and I shall make this offering to you."

Leopard listened with her eyes and her ears. Then she spoke wisely, "If I were a thief, which I am not, I would take your gift. But I cannot do that, as there is one greater than I."

"Who could that be?" asked the woman in desperation.

"It is my teacher."

"Who is that?" questioned the woman.

"That is the one who first taught me to climb trees and how to make the little thunder in my throat. The one who showed me how to slip in and out of shadows, and how to keep my spots clean. The one who is craftier than Fox and more tenacious than Goat."

The woman asked, "Who could this be?"

Leopard grumbled, "The one to whom you must now offer the kitten."

"Who?" the woman pleaded.

And Leopard said, "Cat."

Comeback Cats

The time comes when the adored cat, the favorite dog, the best friend is ready to take leave of us. The problem is, many of us don't know when, or how, to let go.

In our case, returning from a vacation last year, we received the news that our twenty-year-old Siamese cat was dying, as was our ten-year-old Great Dane. The moment they had chosen, our absence, was in sync with their own inner rhythm, and it explained why we had been having lucid dreams of being with them, night after night. Our trip was a bit haunted with ghostly appearances of Moonie and Zeb. They stood before us, as if impatient with our being away, and they tried to tell us in the best way they knew to come back from wherever we were, now. We heard them, we responded—but not quite soon enough.

With heart medicine, we kept Zeb for another well-spent month. Moonie, cat to the end, left more abruptly. We buried him in the back yard, and Gerald placed a circlet of pine cones around the earthen mound. Then he lamented the time that Moonie had chosen to die some months earlier. He, Moonie, had gone off into the impenetrable palmettos during a rainstorm and had not returned all that day and into the night. He had willed himself to die his own way, in the woods, in secrecy, all alone. Somehow that was more than we could bear, and Gerald and I called him back pitifully, crying his name into the tall columns of dark pines until, at dusk, stiff and barely able to walk, he returned, mewing like a kitten.

Well, that was his time and we had chosen to push it off, to bypass his own exit and to choose one of our own. How much we miss Moonie becomes more poignant each day, each week, each passing month. He was one cat in a million, a cat person whose personality had been, we thought, rarefied by thousands of lifetimes until, in this last one, he had become a true Buddha-beast—an angel tiger, a princely being whose only thought was for others.

Now, when we pray over his grave, our prayers are always answered.

Over the years we have seen so many animal and human friends, so many loved ones go the way of all flesh that saying goodbye would seem normal, if it were not always at such an unexpected hour.

Our Maxmillian parrot said goodbye one night so quickly we nearly missed it. Gerald had fallen asleep with Clouseau (he had an absurd mustache and a French accent) on his finger, and the bird who had been dying slowly for days woke him up with a last kiss right on the lips and died just like that, a second later. When our blue-fronted Amazon called Captain passed, however, he was just a baby and he called Gerald and me Ma and Pa. It was heartbreaking when he died because he kept crying, "Ma and Pa" over and over in this child-disconsolate, broken voice that begged for help. When Captain was gone, Gerald closed himself off in a room and wept for eight hours.

We had a parakeet named Birdie who sang without stopping for more than twelve years; she was the singingest parakeet we ever had. A few days before Birdie passed, a woman who was dying of cancer visited our home and remarked that the bird seemed to be an angelic spirit. Several days later, the woman succumbed to cancer and we put some of her favorite music, 1930s jazz, on our boom box and toasted her leaving with a glass of wine. Suddenly the front door of our house opened wide and at the same moment, Birdie jumped into the air and fell to the floor of her cage, dead. We've always known that our departed friend, Betty, came back to say goodbye, and that Birdie, whose time had also come, saw her and left with her.

Krebs, our Persian cat of fifteen years, died quietly and gently and with plenty of warning. Frail and exhausted from suffering through a long illness, she could barely move—but she got to her feet, and placed a trembling paw over my lips. Then she closed her large green eyes and left. But not without returning. Krebs was not one to leave without a ripple. She enjoyed entrances and exits almost as much as she liked to be a foil for our dogs. Therefore, we saw her spirit several times before she finally decided it was time to go to move on to the next experience.

Once, when we were having a particularly hard time financially and we were praying for financial assistance, we saw a cat that looked exactly like Krebs. Thinking it was she, we followed the small dark shadow as it disappeared behind a clump of juniper bushes. Under that gnarled and twisted tree, which had a trunk four feet around and was many centuries old, we found something her spirit had meant for us to see. It was a dark Madonna carved out of volcanic rock and belonging to the Pueblo. Presumably it had been hidden in the valley some five hundred years earlier. Within days of finding this sacred object, which we returned to a contemporary kiva shortly after, work opportunities began to trickle in, then pour in, and our monetary burdens were seemingly over.

There is no easy way to say goodbye. There is no metaphysical cat blessing that works every time; just as there is no guarantee, as the wise man said, that the caterpillar will turn into a butterfly. Emily Brontë, author of *Wuthering Heights*, said that only the strongest of human spirits go beyond the grave and return rapaciously, like Heathcliff, looking for something lost, or bringing something found. In any event, we know that certain of our animal people come back to comfort us, like Mocha the Akita, who hated and feared nothing except gunshots and thunder. One night, days after her death, we had a momentous Florida thunderstorm that shook the foundation of our house.

As white lightning scarred the blackened sky, we thought only of Mocha, and how, one night, she had clawed her way through a closed window, collapsing the wooden frame, to get inside where it was safe. That night, as Gerald and I sat holding hands in the darkened living room, we heard Mocha attack the screen and then paw furiously at the frame. Presently, though the thunder grew louder, she grew quieter, and we said aloud, "There, there, Mocha old girl, you don't have to be frightened any more."

Gerald stood at the window comforting an immaterial and nearly invisible dog; I couldn't see her that clearly but I could, when the flashes burned the sky so brightly, distinguish something of her old form. She was there all right— worried not for herself, as we came to understand after all the years—but for our safety. She'd come back across time to . . . well, to stay a storm for us, to be of comfort for the ones she loved. Mocha remained with us, in spirit, for a few more stormy nights, then she left, and thunder weather behind her, she's not returned.

Catwatch

We now take for granted that cats see in dimensions altogether different from ours, and whether they have color or black-and-white vision, is not as important as their quality of sight. The cat's-eye view is something that humans have long pondered over.

What is a cat's eyeful, anyway? A sundial of the seasons, the hours, the minutes of the moon, as the ancients said. A timepiece most perfectly reflecting tide, incoming and outgoing, they proclaimed. A watch—a catwatch—they decided.

Yet we still have only a vague notion of what the cat really sees when it is in the act of seeing/thinking/being.

Will we ever know, for sure?

To these and other scientific questions, we must smile and shrug, for even if we have confirming evidence of thus-and-so cat sight, what good is it? Can it reveal the hidden mind of the cat? Well, only the cat can do that, and the blessed cat shall not, thank God.

Seeing is being.

Which is to say, the way in which we see, rather than sight itself, is the thing. Moreover, it's the thing that separates us, as humans, from the rest of the animal world. Scientifically, we may learn what the shape of the human skull offers as opposed to the skull of the feline, and how our orbs are situated in that particular casement, but this will not instruct us in the minutiae and magnitude of cat sight.

To do that, we would have to climb inside the feline brain and report what's there. Even then, our insight would only be that, ours. Zen masters have spoken about the vision of cats. Zen sight, they say, is *in*-sight. When Zen abbot Philip Whalen said, "The dog writes on the window with his nose," he meant just that, and more. Seeing is being.

Toonces, the reckless *Saturday Night Live* feline, wouldn't be nearly so funny if we didn't think that, given hands, a cat would, and could, drive a car—and yes, perhaps right over a cliff. What the cat might see, in other words, might compel it to do just that, while our vision requires us to do the opposite.

Some years ago a Zen monk pointed at a tree near where we stood, and said, "How many lizards do you see in that tree?" We answered, "None," for we saw none at all. He responded, "Look more deeply." We did, and gradually, the green iguanas began to come out of camouflage and to appear as starkly defined living things. In an hour of looking, we counted five; but the Zen man saw more, he counted seven. We got to six, never seven.

On another occasion, staying at a house by the sea in Jamaica, we noticed that, each morning, a man or woman hung some freshly washed clothes on the line. We could see the clothes after they were placed to dry, but not as they were being hung out—for it was just too far for the human eye to see, a couple of miles at least. However, in the course of one week while steadily perusing the line at the same hour every morning, we began to make out certain details.

Eventually, we saw a human shape, a vague, impressionistic, shadowy form hanging out the wet clothes. At the end of another week, we were able to focus on the man's—it was not a woman's—hands, an accomplishment considering at the start of the vacation, we could make out nothing except the clothes. Too many months, we decided, with eyes glued to a computer screen.

Now, take this to where it leads: perception. Grant four or five thousand years of finely tuned perception to the formidable-seeing feline, the head-bobbing owl, the osprey, the eagle. Add to this the God-given lenses that work magnificently at a distance, and of course the predisposition to use them for the hunt, and maybe you have something—just a little inkling—of transspecies vision, in particular, cat sight.

The American Zen poet Gary Snyder, says it so well in "this poem is for birds."

> Black swifts.
> —the swifts cry
> As they shoot by, See or go blind!

Isn't that something similar to the cat? See or go blind? And the swift and the cat, as a result of conditioning, see really, really well.

Snyder, speaking of the clear mind, the brain emptied of meaning in his poem "Piute Creek":

> All the junk that goes with being human
> Drops away, hard rock wavers
> Even the heavy present seems to fail

This bubble of a heart.
Words and books
Like a small creek off a high ledge
Gone in the dry air.

And then, in the same poem, the poet goes cat-like, and imagines the night vision of a visitor to his camp:

A clear, attentive mind
Has no meaning but that
Which sees is truly seen.
No one loves rock, yet we are here.
Night chills. A flick
In the moonlight
Slips into juniper shadow:
Back there unseen
Cold proud eyes
Of Cougar or Coyote
Watch me rise and go.

Using Zen as a metaphor for beyond-human reasoning, traveling into the land of no-reason and into pure unadulterated sight reminds us of the critic who once scolded Jack Kerouac for his novel *Desolation Angels*, calling it the view of a "Buddhist Norman Rockwell." This, said thirty years ago, was supposed to be biting; today it rings true and is wholly complimentary.

Kerouac, like Whalen and Snyder, had a special affinity, it would seem, for understanding the feline world, if only because cats see things differently, and their being is encased in seeing.

This morning, we watched Kit Kat beg for her favorite dish of Salmon Feast, which I duly rendered up. However, by the time the sun was up and the dish was revealed and the smell of the salmon reached her nostrils, her senses were given to something else.

A small rabbit, hunched like a brown stone on the edge of the property, had aroused her; her little frame was arched and she was twittering at the tail. Her entire magnetic being was compressed into a single-eyed predatory cat. She was, it seemed, all eye. And what brain there was registered, not food, as we might imagine, but merely rabbit. Once let out, she stalked said rabbit, missed a hit, came back in but had no interest in eating, and so went to sleep. Perhaps the dream of the hunt was more propitious than the doing of it. Anyway, we shall never know.

Yet, one dreams, too, of owning that eye, of living in it for a moment like the man who was dying of a viper bite, who said, "I think now I can see with the eyes of a serpent." Asked after he recovered what that sight was like, he said, "It was all askew, non-human, violet light, very abstract, but I sensed every-

thing around me for miles and
miles; I was, I believe, my
environment."

Oh, what we'd do for an
eye of cat, one little look into the land of look behind,
through, in, and around. That would be a lot more
interesting than seven lizards in a tree.

Catspeak

We asked our cousin Kyle, the cat maven, if she thought all cats could speak.

"You mean, in our language, or theirs?"

"Well, let's say, ours."

She pursed her lips and her blue eyes got very thoughtful, and she replied, "Not all cats talk our way—some do, some don't—but most cats can communicate with us their way."

By which she meant telepathically. She was right, of course. Some cats—Moonie, for instance—spoke the King's English. In fact, a writer asked us the other day whether she could add Moonie to a book she was writing about cat communication, and she

asked us whether Moonie spoke in well-defined syl-
lables. Well, he was a Siamese and they are notable
talkers, vowelers, you might say, for that is the way
they vocalize—in nicely rounded and inflected
vowels.

Occasionally, Moonie used to keep us awake at
night, telling us about all the animal and human spirits that were passing through our house. Then he
would wander off and talk about what a bad day he'd
had, the lousy sleep he'd gotten (or rather, not gotten) and so on and so forth until we asked him to
please put a lid on it. Which he always did . . . eventually. He could talk, no doubt about it. Of course,
that is the reputation of the Siamese—as the conver-
sationalists of the princes and princesses of Siam.

Kyle speaks to her Mo and other cats of hers in a
kind of funny pidgin English sort of thing that was a
language Hemingway used with the cats he called
"cotsies." He spoke to bears and other animals, too.
And why not? What arrogance—to imagine that animals cannot understand human speech. How they
choose to answer us—or not—is their business.

In so many ways, animals behave just as we do.
We have seen long-eared New Mexican hares square
off and box by Queensberry rules, while the maiden
bunny sat on a stone, watching to see whom the

winner would be. We've seen bald eagles kissing and snakes hugging.

Some years ago when we were having ant trouble—they were all over our kitchen—a Native American friend told us to go outside, find the nest, and make an offering to appease the ants. Then he said, "Tell them they are not to come into the house any more."

"And that will work?" we asked.

"If you give them the right offering."

For a week or more, we gave those annoying ants all kinds of things which they summarily rejected. So, we got to feeling that they were being picky on purpose; that they intended to violate our house no matter what we did.

We told this to our friend.

He laughed, and said, "Give them something they will want again and again."

Well, as it turned out, we had some marijuana seeds and we put one of these at the top of the ant hill, and the next day it was gone, and we left another; and the day after that, it was gone, too. During this time, the ants abandoned our house completely. It went on this way until we were out of seeds and then we saw a little blue bead sitting on top of the mound. We showed it to our friend, who said, "It's turquoise from a long time ago. Nice trade."

We think all animals, all creatures, are talking to us all the time, but mostly, we're not listening. Too busy with other things. The other day, in Jamaica, we sat on our verandah and just listened to the birds. There were many kinds of small quits, banana quits and grass quits mostly, flying around the property while talking about their lives on the wing. We found a suitable way to let them know we were listening, and would like to get into the conversation. This consisted of a reedy, whispery, hissy noise that sounded like a flat, aerated whistle. For one long moment, every bird on the grounds was silent.

And then they all started to talk at once. It was as if there were a thousand conversations going on at the same time, with every winged person wanting to join in. This went on for days on end, to the surprise of some of our friends.

However, it wasn't surprising to us—we have resident redbirds in Florida that sing us awake and carry on avid repartees most of the day. They do, in fact depend on us to talk to them, and they get worried when we're unduly quiet. And, we know for a fact that they've told other birds about us because they, too, have come around to chat at various times and to see if we can whistle in their dialect, too.

Naturally, some varieties of birdspeak are impossible for human lips to essay; nonetheless, we do try.

Sometimes our listeners fly off at our first attempt; sometimes they actually laugh at us, but usually our futile attempt is followed by a stunned silence. On occasion, we've offended a bird friend and driven him or her off the property with our impropriety.

But back to cats. If your cat doesn't speak to you, it might signify that your interests do not lie in the area of trans-species communication. Because cats can and will talk our way; and we can do the tele-pathic thing with them whenever we're so inclined. Kit Kat is silent, in terms of human speech, but her telepathy is loud and clear. We were testing her the other morning, showing her powers of understanding to our granddaughter, by telling her in English that we were going to give her a big kiss and a hug—some-thing she detests. Off she went, every time we said it. Finally, we struck up a deal. We said, "We're going to kiss you just once, and in exchange, we're going to give you a bowl of fresh salmon. She leapt into our arms. Our granddaughter was impressed. She asked, "But how do you do catspeak *her* way?"

We told her, "Like this," whereupon Gerald told Kit Kat in his mind that he was going to let her out-doors to chase a rabbit. Instantly, she went for the glass slider and waited there until one of us opened it. But when we got outside to the lanai, which is screened in and there was yet another door, Gerald sent this mental message, "I am not going to open the outside door because, as you see, the rabbit is gone." Kit Kat lay down behind the barbecue grill, and went to sleep.

The world speaks to us in many ways and in many tongues. We have never written an animal book without the permission, or perhaps it might be more truthful to say, the authorship of a telepathic animal, usually the animal to whom or about whom the book is written. Kit Kat has blessed this one a few times, so has Beeper the dachshund,  Hilly and Gray the Great Danes—although, come to think of it, Hilly has been bumping our elbows a lot lately while we've been typing. Do you think she's trying to tell us something?

The Blessing of the Christmas Cat

Who is to say that the wondrous cat cannot fly? And that the gift of movement does exceed even "the face of the earth" that Christopher Smart attributes to him, and thus cover the upper realms as well? Knowing that "God is his Savior" the gentle and ubiquitous cat goes everywhere—to the four corners of the globe, passing through air, earth, water, and fire and proving that God has truly "blessed him in the variety of his movements."

Thus, this tale to close the year and pass the blessing along—for just as cats were once proof against the sinking ship (and insurance companies would not sign policies of transport ships without a cat on deck), so they are also the proven guardians of the air.

According to an old cat myth, a mother cat was present when baby Jesus was born. In the dove-cooing softness of the manger, kittens were born and a mother cat did purr. And, it is said, this sound filled the manger with a song of blessing.

There are, indeed, many stories of this kind, proving the love of Jesus Christ for animals, especially cats. One such tale tells how Jesus found a young cat on the road during one of his pilgrimages. The cat had suffered terribly from neglect, but Jesus spoke soothing words to her, and he carried her to a village and saw to it that she was well fed. Afterward, he gave the unfortunate cat to one of his disciples, a poor widow, who asked the Master a question.

"Is this not some lost sister, that you love her so?"

Jesus replied, "Verily, she has come from the great household of the Father. And whosoever cares for her and gives her food and drink in her need, shall do the same unto me."

Perhaps this story crossed the mind of the great explorer Lincoln Ellsworth, in 1935, as he flew over Antarctica nearly two thousand years after the birth of the Savior. Traveling across a frozen world, untouched and even unsought by humanity,

Ellsworth must have wondered what had brought him there on such a lonely mission. For it was Christmas Eve, and as he looked down at the glittering wastes below his wings, he saw that the land was unfit for man or beast and the coldness of it penetrated his very soul.

However, over the airplane's steady drone, he seemed to hear another, gentler roar. This was the  solitary purr of the cat he carried with him on this, the first twenty-three hundred mile, single-engine airplane flight over the Antarctic. He glanced at the box wherein the cat was stretched out and, to his surprise, he saw there were kittens there too. Thus, the kindness of Jesus was passed on that most holy night, over a desert of ice and within a shaft of hurtling steel two thousand years after the first Christmas purr was heard by the dreaming infant in the manger of Bethlehem.

Pawscript: Alone in the Ninth House

We received a letter the other day from a writer friend named Karen, who is grieving over her ailing cat. She wrote that her poor feline, suffering from cancer, climbed atop our book *The Mythology of Cats*, and slept there for several hours. Karen thought this was a sign and wrote to us. Her letter is one of many, for people write often about their animals, but particularly about suffering, dying, and even dead cats. These gentle souls want some solace, some word that might comfort them and their feline friends.

However, there is not much that can be said except that cats die very differently from other animals we have known. And their time of death, their choice of the precise hour or second, is a thing of much mysticism. The release of the ninth life? It seems so. How beautiful the cat's artful coming, how precious the slow or sudden going. We, who remain at bedside or roadside, are left bereft. But we are often touched by our friend's last gesture because there is frequently a message in it, or shortly thereafter, a gesture of wisdom magically revealed.

The friend whose dying cat climbed onto our book wrote to us the other day to say that her cat passed and that she couldn't get used to her absence. It pained her so. We told her that, by and by, she would see or hear her friend again because "the cat always comes back," and this one did, apparently, two days later. Karen wrote us and said her feline friend, Little Man, came back to scratch in his cat box one last time before going on forever. She said she heard the pawing and scratching, like no other sound really, and she knew it was Little Man and that that was his way of saying goodbye.

Some time ago, another friend, Alicia, wrote to us that a cat she did not know entered her bedroom and tore around like an agitated, invisible whirlwind. This happened early in the morning, before first light, and she was horrified. The twisting whorl of hot, phantom air lasted for about fifteen minutes. Alicia said she had gotten up on her bed and was standing there, screaming, "Get out! Get out!" She opened her bedroom window, and finally in a blast of leaf-stirring frenzy, the supernatural cat exited into the night of cottonwood autumn, and left Alicia very shaken, sobbing, and calling for help.

The next morning, in the bright sunshine, she was sure that the whole thing had been a nightmare, and she wanted no one to know about it. Finally, though, she wrote to us and told us the tale, and we wrote back that we thought the cat's actions were a psychic message to her from someone who had passed on.

She then told us how her father had died. He was one of the scientists who worked on the Manhattan Project, and he had committed suicide. First, he had jumped off a bridge—but he survived. Later, when he jumped off a building, he did not survive.

Was the invisible cat a message from her father? Was he trying to tell her something about the awful end of his life? She believed the cat was "his karmic energy taking leave of the world one last time." Not surprising to those who understand the pattern of family suicide, Alicia took her own life by slipping off the Rio Grande Gorge Bridge, north of Taos, New

Mexico. Her exit was intentional, as she herself said in a letter that explained the pain she was in. The bridge, her father, the whirling dervish cat that spoke to her of disorder and death—all these seemed to have come unraveled in the years since she passed away. There is a pattern to everything, or as Bob Marley put it: "For everything a season/Find its reason."

Why the cat? Why this one subtle creature and not some other of Noah's beauties? Perhaps this unanswerable question is the reason we have such a thing as the metaphysical cat. If the cat has your tongue, you are said to be silenced, but what of the cat itself? Shall she be silenced, too? And we, forever mesmerized by her emptiness, her quiet wonder in the face of disaster, disorder, sorrow, tragedy, comedy, collapse of worlds?

The greatest wonder of all is that, whatever the cat is, we are so much less without her. She helps to complete us, somehow, by filling in that which we lack: the primal sense that life is more than four-square/three-dimension/four-color, that and whatever else you might care to name.

Life is inexhaustible mystery, life is fantasy of the purest kind. What we misname "everyday life" is the greatest dream, the most fantastic fiction one could ever imagine. And we have the cat to tell us just that—to convey that what we don't know is not unknowable, but perhaps just inexpressible or unreachable by eye, ear, nose, and hand. There are, the cat winks reassuringly, the other senses. There are, the cat smiles seductively, the other worlds—those beyond the physical.

Hence, the metaphysical cat.

She who knows no bounds, who dances in dust and snow, who outraces rain and surpasses smoke, who sleeps on trash and velvet, who walks on burning tin and electric wire, the metaphysical cat who hath more than the nine lives conferred by Mohammed, who hath reasons that reason cannot encounter, who is no mere riddle, no small conundrum, but the gateway to the All. And when we see those little footsteps that go we  know not where, we shouldn't lament or be despondent.

In fact, we ought to be thankful for that which we can't, by force of will, encounter; thankful for the door that has no key. We should let something remain as it was and always will be, a mystery. The metaphysical cat, undecodable and irreducible, and usually, unavailable for comment.

Bibliography

A&E's Incredible World of Cats. Gary H. Grossman and Robb Weller, New York: A&E Home Video, 1996.

Altman, Roberta. *The Quintessential Cat*. New York: Macmillan, 1994.

Blake, William. *Songs of Innocence and of Experience*. New York: Oxford University Press, 1986.

Caras, Roger A. *A Celebration of Cats*. New York: Simon and Schuster, 1986.

Cirlot, J. E. *A Dictionary of Symbols*. Translated by Herbert Read, New York: Philosophical Library, 1962.

Conger, Jean. *The Velvet Paw: A History of Cats in Life, Mythology, and Art*. New York: Ivan Obolensky, 1963.

Corey, Paul. *Do Cats Think? Notes of a Cat-Watcher.* Chicago: Henry Regnery, 1977.

Dale-Green, Patricia. *Cult of the Cat.* Boston: Houghton-Mifflin, 1963.

de Caro, Frank, ed. *The Folktale Cat.* New York: Barnes and Noble, 1992.

Duggan, Colm. *Treasures of Irish Folklore.* New York: Arlington House, 1983.

Gay, Margaret Cooper. *How to Live With a Cat.* New York: Simon and Schuster, 1953.

Gettings, Fred. *The Secret Lore of the Cat.* New York: Carol, 1989.

Gilbert, John R. *Cats, Cats, Cats, Cats, Cats, Cats.* London: Paul Hamlyn, 1961.

Graves, Robert. *The White Goddess: A Historical Grammar of Poetic Myth.* New York: Ferrar, Strauss and Cudahy, 1948.

Greene, David. *Incredible Cats.* London: Methun, 1984.

Hamilton, Elizabeth. *Cats, A Celebration*. New York: Scribners, 1979.

Hotchner, A. E. *Papa Hemingway: A Personal Memoir.* London: Simon and Schuster UK ltd, 1999.

Howey, M. Oldfield. *The Cat in Mysteries of Religion and Magic*. London: Bracken, 1993.

Joseph, Michael. *Cat's Company*. London: Hazell, Watson and Viney, 1930.

Kirk, Mildred. *The Everlasting Cat*. Woodstock, NY: Overlook Press, 1977.

Lockridge, Frances and Richard. *Cats and People*. Philadelphia: Lippincott, 1950.

Méry, Fernand. *The Life, History, and Magic of the Cat*. Translated by Emma Street, New York: Grosset and Dunlop, 1969.

Moyes, Patricia. *How to Talk to Your Cat*. New York: Wings, 1993.

Repplier, Agnes. *The Fireside Sphinx*. Boston: Houghton Mifflin, 1901.

Saroyan, William. *Here Comes, There Goes, You Know Who*. New York: Barracade, 1995.

_____. *Tracy's Tiger*. New York: Ballantine, 1967.

Schneck, Marcus, and Jill Caravan. *Cat Facts*. New York: Barnes and Noble, 1990.

Simmons, Eleanor Booth. *Cats*. New York: Whittlesey House, McGraw-Hill, 1935.

Simms, Katharine L. *They Walked Beside Me: A Cat Book in Which Dogs Are Welcome*. London: Hutchinson, 1955.

Thomas, Elizabeth Marshall. *The Tribe of Tiger: Cats and Their Culture*. New York: Simon and Schuster Audioworks, 1994.

Tovey, Doreen. *Cats in the Belfry*. New York: Doubleday, 1958.

Van Vechten, Carl. *The Tiger in the House*. New York: Dorset Press, 1989.

Winslow, Helen M. *Concerning Cats: My Own and Some Others*. New York: Lothrop, 1900.

Wylder, Joseph. *Psychic Pets: The Secret Life of Animals.*
New York: Stonehill, 1978.

Hampton Roads Publishing Company

. . . for the evolving human spirit

Hampton Roads Publishing Company
publishes books on a variety of subjects,
including metaphysics, health, integrative medicine,
visionary fiction, and other related topics.

For a copy of our latest catalog, call toll-free
(800) 766-8009, or send your name and address to:

Hampton Roads Publishing Company, Inc.
1125 Stoney Ridge Road
Charlottesville, VA 22902

hrpc@hrpub.com
www.hrpub.com